Deborah's love of scripture and her desire to see o. [...]ery chapter. While reading this book I was encouraged and excited to dig deeper into Scripture myself. Deborah shows us how even someone with a busy schedule can truly engage in the Word. This is a practical book that is great read for the new believer or someone who has been a Christian for many years.

--R.T. Stringer, Pastor
Villa Baptist Church

In a day and age when biblical literacy is at an all-time low, Deborah Haddix has given us a helpful and practical guide that will encourage you to reengage in your study of the scriptures, or take your study to a new level. As a pastor I am always looking for new tools to help others grow in their study of the scriptures. If you work with others to help them grow in their knowledge of the scriptures or need a little help growing yourself, this is a must have for your library.

--Nate Young, Pastor
Crossbridge Church

Deborah's words are truth-filled, practical, and full of encouragement. She understands how busy our lives are, but she's passionate about making scripture reading and study a priority in the lives of Christian women and gives simple but clear tools to make that a reality. As a busy pastor's wife and homeschooling mother of three, her words are life-giving to me, helping me re-focus and remember the great gift that God has given me in His Word.

--Heather Greene
The King's Chapel, Brooklyn, NY

Psalm 19:7 reminds us, "The law of the Lord is perfect, reviving the soul." That's good news, isn't it? But, God's Word has little value to us if we are not reading it slowly, carefully, personally. Deborah Haddix serves us well in giving us such insightful, practical suggestions on how to read the Word of God and apply its divinely inspired content to our lives. This short book is worth your time.

--Larry E. McCall, Author
Walking Like Jesus Did and *Grandparenting with Grace*

The Word of God changes lives just as much today as it ever has. The power is in the Scriptures that have been preserved for us. Deborah does a remarkable job challenging us to make it a priority to be engaged in God's Word, and she resources us with practical ways to make Scripture a necessary part of our every moment. This book is a must read for people in all areas of their spiritual journey.

--Chuck Smith, Pastor
The Valley Church

Engaging the Scripture:

ENCOUNTERING GOD

IN THE PAGES OF HIS WORD

Susan,
Thank you, thank you!
I can't begin to say it
all here — sounding
board, encourage,
reader, FRIEND!
Thank you for seeing
me through again.
Love,
Debbie

Engaging the Scripture:

ENCOUNTERING GOD

IN THE PAGES OF HIS WORD

Deborah Haddix

For Don,
who knows me best
yet chooses each day to stay right here and share the journey.

CONTENTS

ACKNOWLEDGMENTS

I am especially grateful and extend my heartfelt thanks to…

Susan Borgstrom, Sherry Schumann, and Kim Young – sounding boards, encouragers, and readers beyond compare. Your faithfulness, patience, and prayers are a gift. Thank you for all the little things and for the many hours you devoted to reading through drafts and providing input.

Glenda Taylor – editor extraordinaire, who selflessly and enthusiastically donated her time, talent, and expertise to helping this book take shape. I treasure your thoroughness, attention to detail, diligence, and most of all, your friendship.

Betsy Abraham – whose organizational skills and administrative support enabled me to remain focused on the writing process. Thank you for your willingness to do "whatever" and for so graciously and eagerly stepping into the role of Book Launch Manager.

Micki Krieger, Samantha Franklin, Amber Miller, Roberta Vinyard, Crystal Clair, Julia Sykes, Melissa Waters, Jill P Jones, Susan Block, Glenice Hall, Ann Ferri, Vicki Gabbard, Lillian Penner, Karen Kaynan, Kim Young, Mary Sowjanya, Joy Young, Patty Glumack, Amy Ballard, Kelli Holeyfield, Shelly Dawes, Ashley Rasico, Deborah Cruz, Brenda Chatham, Vanessa Oliver, Myra Cox, Catherine Deputy, Jenn Curry, Glenda Taylor, Nancy Grunkemeyer, Sylvia Thornburg, Melissa Barnes, Barbara Scott, Linda Cabiness, Barbara Kennedy, Sherry Schumann – a community of "sisters" who love the Lord, His Word, and other women.

Don – my husband and cheerleader, whose words of affirmation, encouragement, input, and prayers help me stay the course. May we finish well, together!

FOREWARD

I am very happy to commend this excellent book which presents a holistic picture of Scripture engagement, and offers a wide variety of ways for us to interact with the Word of God. It will challenge individual Christians to discover and/or rediscover the wonders of God's Word, in addition to being an invaluable resource for churches grappling with biblical illiteracy among members, as well as promoting the Bible and its message in the public sphere.

The need for such a resource is critical. Roughly one in three Americans (31%) report they never read the Bible, and a further 24% read it three or four times a year or less often. Only one in six adults (16%) say they engage the Bible every day while a further 14% do so several times a week.[1] In other large English-speaking countries – Canada, the UK, and Australia – the incidence of Bible reading is probably considerably lower.

This contrasts with the global South and East where a great hunger for God's Word is found in a range of countries and among many indigenous people groups. There, the supply of Bibles cannot keep pace with the rapid church growth to such an extent that some Christian communities are facing 'Bible poverty.' In contrast many Christians in Western countries appear to have succumbed to a spiritual anorexia apparent in a reluctance to read and inwardly digest the Bible with any degree of regularity. In the UK, 1 in 6 church attenders have confessed to never reading anything in the Bible in their entire churchgoing life. While research in New Zealand has revealed that 3 out of 4 church attenders read the Bible only occasionally or hardly ever.

The recovery of biblical literacy is one of the urgent needs confronting many churches in the West. Being biblically literate is more than knowing the Bible's contents. I like to define Biblical Literacy as the ability to inhabit, understand, interpret, and communicate the master story of Holy Scripture.[2] Biblical literacy is rounded insofar as there is mutual engagement between our whole personality (mind and heart) and the whole Bible

---

[1] *Scripture Engagement: State of the Bible 2019*, a report of a nationwide study in the USA, commissioned by the American Bible Society and conducted by the Barna Group (https://www.americanbible.org/state-of-the-bible).

[2] This statement is modelled in part on UNESCO's understanding that basic literacy is a learning process. 'Beyond its conventional concept as a set of reading, writing and counting skills, literacy is now understood as a means of identification, understanding, interpretation, creation, and communication in an increasingly digital, text-mediated, information-rich and fast-changing world.' (https://en.unesco.org/themes/literacy, downloaded May 9, 2019).

(Genesis to Revelation). Too often our engagement with Scripture is a purely intellectual exercise in which analysis for information trumps a desire for transformation. And in our Bible reading we tend to marginalise large sections of the Bible, despite Paul assuring us that 'all Scripture' is 'useful for teaching the truth, rebuking error, correcting faults, and giving instruction in right living' (2 Tim. 3:16, GNT).[3] Biblical literacy, like basic literacy, is a learning process in which we intentionally explore a biblical passage, employing both left brain and right brain, with an openness for the Holy Spirit drawing us into the text so that we internalize it in who we are and actualize it in what we do.

Becoming biblically literate means taking Scripture engagement seriously and making it a priority. This book by Deborah Haddix challenges and equips us precisely to do this. It explains five basic ways of engaging with God's Word: reading it, writing it, meditating on it, memorizing it, and praying it, while stressing that Scripture engagement is a relational process which at times can become a struggle. Many will find particularly helpful the personal reflection and resources sections that conclude each chapter.

Scripture engagement is vital for three main reasons:

First, the triune God reveals himself to us in Scripture. The Old Testament Scriptures are God the Father's testimony to his Son. The Scriptures of both Testaments are the sceptre with which Christ mediates his Lordship over the church. And the Holy Spirit who in time past inspired the writers of Scripture, today animates the sacred text so that God speaks to us through it.

Second, the *Reveal* research conducted over three years (2004-2007) on 250,000 people at 1,000 North American churches yielded hard evidence that Scripture engagement is the most powerful catalyst for spiritual growth. The study explored 50 different factors that impact spiritual growth (defined as loving God and loving others). Here is a key finding: "Nothing has a greater impact on spiritual growth than reflection on Scripture. *If churches could do only one thing to help people at all levels of spiritual maturity grow in their relationship with Christ, their choice is clear. They would inspire, encourage, and equip their people to read the Bible—specifically, to reflect on Scripture for meaning in their lives.*"[4]

---

[3] A survey by Crossway on which sections of the Bible are most read and hardest to understand, reports that only 15% of respondents include the Old Testament books as read most often compared with 85% who mostly read the New Testament (*FutureFirst*, April, 2019).

[4] *Move: What 1,000 Churches Reveal About Spiritual Growth*, by Greg Hawkins and Cally Parkinson (p. 19).

Third, there is no human task more missionally strategic today than Christians engaging with and submitting to Scripture as the sceptre of Christ, and then sharing their experience with unbelievers. For according to Jesus, the Word is the seed that, as it is sown, will advance God's Kingship in our lost and broken world.

As you engage with Scripture, why not make the psalmist's wish *your* prayer: 'Let me see clearly so that I may take in the amazing things from your law' (Ps. 119:18, *Voice* translation).

--Dr. Fergus Macdonald
Taylor University Center for Scripture Engagement
Chair of the Scottish Evangelical Theology Society
Chair Emeritus of the Forum of Bible Agencies International

1

God's Great Gift

The Bible is one of God's greatest gifts to His people.

Filled with declarations of His nature, it is the very Word of our living and ever-present God. The Bible is a powerful miracle that has been safeguarded for generations. It is our tool and companion in coming to know God.

This gift—Scripture—is vital to soul nourishment.

Second Timothy 3:16 tells us, *"All Scripture is breathed out by God...."* Breathed by Him, it is His very Word recorded and preserved for us.

Additionally, a look through the pages of the Bible reveals much more evidence to the necessity of Scripture to our soul's good health:

- **God speaks to us through Scripture:**
  "Long ago, at many times and in many ways, God spoke to our fathers by the prophets, but in these last days he has spoken to us by his Son, whom he appointed the heir of all things, through whom also he created the world."
  Hebrews 1:1-2

- **The words of the Bible are living and active:**
  "For the word of God is living and active, sharper than any two-edged sword, piercing to the division of soul and of spirit, of joints and of marrow, and discerning the thoughts and intentions of the heart. And no creature is hidden from his sight, but all are naked and exposed to the eyes of him to whom we must give account." Hebrews 4:12-13

- **Scripture revives our soul and makes the truth known:**
  "The law of the Lord is perfect, reviving the soul; the testimony of the Lord is sure, making wise the simple." Psalm 19:7

- **It equips us for service:**
  "All Scripture is breathed out by God and profitable for teaching, for reproof, for correction, and for training in righteousness, that the man of God may be complete, equipped for every good work." 2 Timothy 3:16-17

- **The words of Scripture form us into one who can stand strong in the battle:**
  "For we do not wrestle against flesh and blood, but against the rulers, against the authorities, against the cosmic powers over this present darkness, against the spiritual forces of evil in the heavenly places." Ephesians 6:12

- **The Bible instructs us, encourages us, and helps us endure.**
  "For whatever was written in former days was written for our instruction, that through endurance and through the encouragement of the Scriptures we might have hope." Romans 15:4

- **It helps us come to know God:**
  "And this is eternal life, that they know you, the only true God, and Jesus Christ whom you have sent." John 17:3

Spend some additional time in Psalm 119, a chapter replete with the benefits of Scripture! In this one chapter alone, you will find that Scripture nourishes the soul (v. 25), convicts (v. 29), redirects our wayward gaze (v. 37), fills us with hope (v. 49), comforts (v. 50), prompts our praise (v. 62), reassures (v. 75), fosters love (v. 97), leads to wisdom (v. 100), feeds the hungry soul (v. 103), strengthens the weary (v. 107), guards and protects (v.

115), assures us of our inheritance (v. 123), lifts the discouraged (v. 147), and offers peace (v. 165).

All this and more are true of this precious gift of Scripture. Yet perhaps the chief reason the Bible is crucial to the nourishing of our soul is that when we spend time in Scripture, we encounter God. In fact, every time we come to the Bible, we can meet God; we can come to know Him more.

Spending time in the Bible is like stepping into God's house; we can learn so much about Him by visiting his "home." Similarly, if you were to step into my house, you would learn much about me from what you notice there. For instance, the many books on the shelves would tell you that I enjoy reading. Toys and sippy cups would be indicators that young children are frequently in my home, and all the photos of my family on display would speak of their value to me. It is the same with the Bible. Everything is there, within its pages, because God desires it to be.

The Importance of Scripture to Jesus

Not only is Scripture of utmost importance to us today, God's Word tells us of its significance to Jesus as He walked this earth:

> *"But he answered, 'It is written, "'Man shall not live by bread alone, but by every word that comes from the mouth of God.'"* Matthew 4:4

In essence, Scripture provided His life mission statement. Through it, He was strengthened to resist Satan's temptations and taught to compose the Lord's Prayer. Scripture inspired His wisdom and helped Him to endure the agony of the cross. It was Jesus' intimacy with God's words that empowered Him to overcome by the love of the Father and the power of the Spirit.

Just as Scripture was of most importance to Jesus as He walked the earth, it is vital to the health of our soul today. Whether we truly understand just how vital, most of us desire to spend time in God's Word. As children of the King, we want to know His will and to have His Word inform our lives. We want to know Him and to live transformed lives. Yet, we struggle.

Personal Reflection

1. This chapter is filled with the necessities or benefits of Scripture to the health of our soul. Step into "God's house" by opening your Bible to some of the verses listed in this chapter. What do these Scriptures tell you about God?

2. Spend time daily filling your mind with Scripture:

   - Open your Bible to Psalm 119 or Psalm 19.

   - Sit with the Scripture and read straight through the passage.

   - Pull up an audio version and listen as the words are read aloud to you.

   - Print out a copy and highlight each "benefit" of Scripture.

3. In your current life season, how do the following verses and Jesus' example speak to you about the importance of Scripture?

   "For the word of God is living and active, sharper than any two-edged sword, piercing to the division of soul and of spirit, of joints and of marrow, and discerning the thoughts and intentions of the heart." Hebrews 4:12

   "Let the word of Christ dwell in you richly, teaching and admonishing one another in all wisdom, singing psalms and hymns and spiritual songs, with thankfulness in your hearts to God." Colossians 3:16

4. Pray. Ask God to fill you with a hunger and thirst for His Word, to reveal your areas of struggle with Bible reading, and to open your heart and mind to this precious spiritual discipline.

2

The Struggle is Real!

The struggles we face when it comes to reading the Bible are wide and varied; nevertheless, they are real. College students, marrieds, moms with toddlers and those with teens, members of the work force, empty-nesters, and grandparents, whatever our stage of life, we struggle.

For most of us, time is the obstacle. Our busy schedules filled with family, school, work, ministry, and other life obligations cause our heads to spin and wear us completely out. It seems unfathomable to even consider squeezing one more thing into our day.

Honestly, we can't imagine fitting in time to attend an organized, led-by-someone-else type of Bible study or even sitting down to study or read Scripture in the quiet solitude of our own home.

As a teen-ager, I remember hearing predictions that computers and advanced technology would one day turn our world upside down, providing us with shorter work weeks. In this new predicted age of leisure, we would have unheard of amounts of time for improving our minds, enjoying recreation, and resting our bodies.

I think of those predictions from time to time as I sit to plan my week, thoughtfully considering how to fit study, play, and exercise into an overcrowded schedule. Looking back and looking around, I think it's safe to say those predictions from my younger years were way off the mark.

Time is not the only obstacle when it comes to reading the Bible. Another struggle faced by many is the "why" of reading. Some read the Bible purely out of a sense of duty or obligation. For them, reading Scripture is something to check off a to-do list.

Simply another item added to the day's already packed agenda, this vital spiritual discipline quickly becomes viewed as a chore. Sadder still, some read the Bible as a set of rules – rules which restrict and bind and heap up feelings of failure because on our own we are powerless to keep them.

Others struggling with Bible reading experience the feeling of being ill-equipped for the task. Instructed for years that reading the Bible is important but never taught how to do so, these readers haven't a clue where to begin in reading it for themselves. Intimidated, and convinced they are unable to understand what they read, these Bible readers succumb to mere surface readings or even worse, no reading at all.

Since diving into this topic of how to engage with Scripture, I've heard from many people. Younger, older; women, men; new to the faith, walking in it for years; each one echoing the same frustration. As I think on the wide-spread sentiment of people not knowing HOW to read the Bible for themselves, I find myself wondering if there might not be other contributing factors in addition to the lack of teaching on the subject.

Think about it with me for a moment. We live in an age where we have easier access to the Bible than ever before. However, it's also an age where we are not required to do much or even any of the "reading" work for ourselves. For those whose schedules permit, organized Bible studies abound. Similarly, most churches offer Sunday School, communities, or small groups of various types.

Even if we can't fit those into our weekly plan, we do make it a point to get to church to hear the Pastor preach most Sunday mornings. Christian-authored books abound, and thanks to technology, blog posts, internet articles, and podcasts can be accessed with a few simple clicks. Could it be that in the busyness of our days and the ease with which we can "read" the Word, that we are not developing the ability to read effectively on our own?

A recent LifeWay Research study seems to bear this out. According to their representative survey of 1,000 Americans, almost nine out of ten households (87 percent) own a Bible. Yet more than half of Americans have read little or none of it, and a third never pick it up on their own. Additionally, less than a quarter of those who have ever read a Bible have a systematic plan for reading the Christian Scriptures each day.

The study also found a number of reasons that keep Americans from reading the Bible. According to LifeWay's research, about a quarter (27 percent) say they don't prioritize it, while fifteen percent don't have time. [1]

I would venture to say that most of us "read" the Bible in some of these same ways that have been mentioned: participating in an organized Bible study, attending Sunday School or a small group, hearing the Pastor's Sunday morning sermon, reading books by Christian authors, perusing blog posts or internet articles written by Christians, or listening to podcasts. And these are all good things.

However, I would like to point out that they all have a common denominator, one that would suggest that these types of Bible "reading" are not sufficient on their own.

Do you see it? The common denominator running through this list?

Yes, each one is a passive form of reading involving someone else's interpretation of Scripture.

The Bible is God's chosen way for speaking to us. It is His very Word breathed out and protected for us for centuries – in order that He might speak to us… now, in this century… to each one of us – and we are basically playing "telephone" with it.

Do you remember the game of "telephone?" It was a message-passing game. Someone would start a message around a large circle by whispering into the ear of their neighbor. The message would then continue around the circle, each person whispering what they heard into the ear of the next. When the message finally rested upon the one remaining set of ears in the circle, that person would share the message aloud. In all the years I played the game, the final declared message never even remotely resembled the original.

It is not my aim to bash these other methods of Bible "reading." There is, in my opinion, absolutely nothing wrong with any of them. Actually, I see them as wonderful benefits of living in this technological age. My caution is, however, that we must take care to use them properly – as supplemental tools rather than as our solitary source of Bible "reading."

At this point, we might do well to remember Martin Luther who is quoted as saying: "The Scriptures are our vineyard in which we should all work." [2]

Taking a Cue from Martin Luther

Martin Luther invested years of his life to study. He began his studies in the fields of the arts and sciences and then moved into a master's study of the law. Eventually while spending time in a monastery, Luther embarked on a course of theological study.

In the 1510's, the study of theology meant little more than studying what the masters had to say about the Bible. Luther, therefore, was expected to do little more than master "the sources" so that he could then point future students to those masters.

Sometime later when Luther was transitioning from student to teacher, a new way of learning emerged. Referred to in the Latin as *ad fontes* meaning, "to the sources," this new method of education encouraged students to go directly to the original (or primary source) rather than relying on secondary sources.

Do you remember writing those term papers back in school? The teacher spent hours of class time teaching the difference between primary and secondary sources. Primary sources, we learned, are contemporary to an event and provide firsthand evidence about a topic.

On the other hand, secondary sources are produced sometime after an event, and not being original to the event are, by reason, flawed to some degree. Then after teaching us the difference, the teacher always required that the term paper include a certain number of sources, always more primary than secondary.

God's Word was written and has been preserved over these many generations, just for us. It is our primary source. All those other ways of "reading" are secondary sources, flawed at least in part, by someone else's interpretation. Secondary sources can absolutely be helpful but should never be our major or only source.

When it comes to our Bible reading, is it, perhaps, time that we declare, as Martin Luther did, back "to the source?"

Personal Reflection

1. When it comes to reading the Bible, which of the following best describe your struggles in your current stage of life?

   - Never seem to have enough time.

   - Busyness.

   - Family, work, and other life obligations.

   - Tend to read the Bible as a set of rules.

   - View Bible reading as a chore, one more thing to cross off the to-do list.

   - Don't understand what I read.

   - Intimated by it.

   - Not sure HOW to read the Bible for meaning.

   - Other. _____

2. Think about how you typically "read" the Bible. Which of the following are true?

   - Participating in an organized, led-by-someone else Bible study.

   - Attending Sunday School, Church community group, or small group study.

- Hearing the Pastor deliver the Sunday morning message.

- Reading books written by Christian authors.

- Perusing blog posts and internet articles written by Christians.

- Listening to podcasts.

3. Reflect on your Bible "reading." Do these methods which rely on someone else's interpretation make up all or most of your Bible "reading?" How much time are you spending "in the source?"

A conversation with a close friend recently convicted me in this area. An avid reader, she confessed that she had of late noticed herself quickly glancing over supporting Scriptures when reading through a Christian-authored book.

Remorseful, she reflected that she probably skimmed over the Scripture because of her familiarity with it but realized that what she was actually doing in that act was giving more attention to man's word than God's Word. As I listened to her confession and reflected upon my own reading life, I realized I was guilty of the same.

It's true that most of us have been taught the difference between primary and secondary sources and the importance of using primary sources. But the question begs to be asked, in our technological, hurry-up world abundantly filled with excellent resources, how many of us get lured into spending more time hearing and studying what OTHERS have to say about theology and the Bible than studying it for ourselves?

Where do you stand? Today, in this season? Do the wonderful, valuable resources that are so readily available to us serve as supplemental tools to your own time in Scripture or have they usurped the primary role? Respond in prayer to what you have discovered.

4. Pray. Give your struggles to the Lord and ask Him to turn your struggles to strengths. Pray that He would open your heart and mind to all He has in store for you.

3

Scripture Engagement

Engaging the Scripture is a relational process. Much more than the mere calling out of words as one's eyes cross the page, it is the primary means by which God engages the believer.

What exactly is Scripture engagement? While there is currently no definitive answer to that question, allow me to share two definitions that I find very helpful.

1. "Scripture engagement is interaction with the biblical text in a way that provides sufficient opportunity for the text to speak for itself by the power of the Holy Spirit, enabling readers and listeners to hear the voice of God and discover for themselves the unique claim Jesus Christ is making upon them." [1]
   Dr Fergus Macdonald of the Taylor University Center for Scripture Engagement

Notice two key things from this definition: the interaction between the Bible text and the reader and the engaging relationship between the reader and God.

2. In *Soul Nourishment,* Scripture engagement is defined: "to study, read, meditate on, be shaped by, and connect with the Person that Scripture proclaims. This practice includes the very familiar spiritual discipline of reading the Bible. It also includes study of the Word, memorization, meditation on Scripture, attending

organized Bible study, praying God's Word, and the journaling of verses and passages along with many other ways of interacting with Holy Scripture." [2]

Here again, is an emphasis on interaction between text and reader and relationship between reader and the person that Scripture proclaims.

No matter how many versions of the definition we might examine, we would notice each one including these key points of interaction and relationship.

When it comes right down to it, isn't that want we long for – a deep, meaningful, and engaging relationship with God? It's what we were created for, the longing of our soul, and it can be developed through interaction with God's Word.

For a better understanding of this relationship-building interaction between text and reader, we need look no further than the Bible itself.

As we go to the "source," we find that the Bible instructs us to:

- meditate on (Joshua 1:8, Psalm 1:2)
- consider (Psalm 119:95)
- dwell in (Colossians 3:16)
- think over (2 Timothy 2:7) and
- look into (James 1:25)

the words of Scripture.

In other words, we are to read intentionally with the purpose of hearing from God, knowing Him, deepening our relationship, and nourishing our soul.

A Relational Process

"And this is eternal life, that they know you, the only true God,
and Jesus Christ whom you have sent." John 17:3

Knowing God is our primary purpose, and Scripture is the channel through which we build our relationship with Him. Engaging with Scripture is a relational process through which we come to know Him. When we open the Bible, we must do so thoughtfully, aware that when we sit with God's Word, we sit with Him.

I've heard it said that the Bible is the only book whose author is always present when one reads it. As we read, we must listen intently, for God is there whispering, "Pay attention. I am here!"

Involving Our Heart and Our Mind

Engaging purposefully and intently with Scripture requires the use of our hearts and minds. The Bible, of course, has much to say on the subject:

- *"Now set your mind and heart to seek the LORD your God."* 1 Chronicles 22:19a

- *"You keep him in perfect peace whose mind is stayed on you, because he trusts in you."* Isaiah 26:3

- *"And you shall love the Lord your God with all your heart and with all your soul and with all your mind and with all your strength."* Mark 12:30

- *"What am I to do? I will pray with my spirit, but I will pray with my mind also; I will sing praise with my spirit, but I will sing with my mind also."* 1 Corinthians 14:15

- *"Do not be conformed to this world, but be transformed by the renewal of your mind, that by testing you may discern what is the will of God, what is good and acceptable and perfect."* Romans 12:2-3

The mind is the gateway to the heart. This is the message of Romans 12:2-3. Transformation is not affected by the mind alone, but by a pathway running from the mind to the heart. Far too often we try to love God with our heart while neglecting the role our mind plays in the process. Understanding and transformation (heart work) come through the mind.

In her book, *Women of the Word*, Jen Wilkin writes, "...finding greater pleasure in God will not result from pursuing more experiences of him, but from knowing him better." [3]

Essentially, a deeper, more intimate relationship with God comes from knowing Him better. And knowing Him is the work of the mind. The knowledge of this mind to heart pathway certainly gives new meaning to the old phrase, "to know Him is to love Him."

Scripture Engagement involves the mind and leads to heart transformation. It is a way of coming to God's Word with an awareness that the Bible is a place for encountering God. Scripture Engagement is also an active process, one that invites us to come directly to the "source," in acts of meditation, consideration, and deep thought. All of which result in transformation of heart and deepening relationship with God.

Personal Reflection

1. Two definitions for the term Scripture Engagement are shared in this chapter. Reflect on them by writing out your thoughts, understanding, and questions.

2. What does the following quote mean to you?

   "Acquiring knowledge about the One we love, for the sake of loving him more deeply, will always be for our transformation," from *Women of the Word* by Jen Wilkin. [4]

3. According to John 17:3, what is eternal life?

4. Recall your experience with Bible reading.

   - Was the importance of Bible reading stressed to you?

   - Were you instructed to read the Bible but never taught how to go about it?

   - Have you, at any time, been given clear instructions regarding the reading process?

   - Were you left to figure out Bible reading on your own, or were you taught to read the Bible for meaning?

5. Pray. Invite the Holy Spirit to fill your mind with knowledge of God. Ask for a transformative work to be done in your life through the mind to heart pathway.

4

Getting a Handle on Distractions

Before we dive into the "how-to" of Scripture Engagement, let's take a moment to address the elephant in the room – distraction.

Let's be honest, there is nothing more discouraging than getting excited about meaningful time in God's Word, carving out the time, devising a plan, and sitting with purpose, only to have your attention diverted and your mind drawn away.

Bible reading, interrupted by the dog's need to go out.

The writing out of Scripture, disrupted by incoming texts and calls.

Meditation on God's Word, broken by thoughts of "What's for dinner?"

While distractions vary, their outcome does not. *Distractions always cause us to turn our attention away from our time in God's Word.*

Knowing what we do about distraction, I think it is safe for us to say that distraction is one of the most commonly faced obstacles to meaningful and consistent time in God's Word.

A prominent issue when it comes to engaging with Scripture, distraction must be understood. The truth is, experiencing distractions during our quiet time is absolutely natural. Distractions are not bad things. They are not "wrong."

Essential to our understanding, as well, is the fact that experiencing distractions during our quiet time does NOT make us a failure. However, this is most often exactly how we do feel.

When we go to our quiet time – planned Scripture Engagement – only to be assaulted over-and-over again by distractions, we tend to throw up our hands in defeat.

"I can't do this!"

"It's too hard."

"I give up!"

Score another one for Satan! He has succeeded in keeping us from this much needed time with God.

Might I suggest that rather than giving up (surrendering the battle ground), we need a plan. A plan for combating our distractions successfully when they arrive, and trust me, they will arrive!

Ideas for Creating a Quiet Time Distraction Plan

1. Prepare ahead.

   If you enjoy morning quiet times, prepare for them the night before by getting all your materials ready. For those who wish to engage with Scripture over their morning coffee or during lunch breaks, be sure your coffee or lunch area is set up and ready to go ahead of time.

2. Scout out a well-suited location.

   Choose a spot that is as free from distraction as possible and then test it out. I once chose a lovely spot in my living room as the place where I would dig in to the Bible. Large windows for providing lots of natural light, my favorite comfy chair, a little side table for my materials. The area was prepared ahead of time, and I looked forward to spending some meaningful time in God's Word in this special spot. When the scheduled time arrived, I sat and began. Very soon I was aware of the loud ticking of the grandfather clock sitting in the corner of the room. Never-before bothered by the ticking of this clock, it's sound quickly drew my mind away from the Word demanding my complete attention. Needless to say, that location was abandoned for one that was better suited.

3. Turn off the technology.

   Before settling down, be sure your phone is silenced. If possible, consider physically removing yourself from things like phones, iPads, computers, and TVs. I realize many people like to use dictionary and Bible help apps when engaging with Scripture. However, it's important to know yourself when you are setting up your Distraction Plan. Are you disciplined enough to avoid incoming calls and texts? Do you easily succumb to chasing rabbit trails? Make provision, as needed, in your plan.

4. Tune out the noise.

   If finding a location with zero to minimal noise distraction is not possible, try using ear plugs or noise-cancelling headphones.

5. Keep a note pad handy.

   As things pop into your mind during your quiet time, simply record them on your note pad. This simple act allows you to acknowledge the distraction and then immediately return your attention to the task at hand. Amazingly, all those distracting thoughts that seem to number in the millions when left in your head, become something much more manageable when corralled on a note pad.

6. Take a walk.

   Fresh air and exercise are always good. However, walking as you pray, reflect, or meditate on Scripture engages your body and helps to keep you focused. Go for a walk at your nearby park, prayer walk around your neighborhood, or walk your yard. If you can't get outside, try walking through your home or pacing around a room.

7. Hydrate.

   It is a simple, yet often overlooked, fact that focus is a difficult thing when our bodies have need. Make yourself comfortable before you begin. Take care of your needs and keep a water bottle handy.

8. Check your posture.

   Before entering your quiet time, take a few minutes to properly posture yourself before the Lord.

   - Get comfortable, but not too comfortable. You don't want to fall asleep.

   - Take a couple of deep, slow breaths.

   - Consciously let go of any tasks and responsibilities.

   - Observe a few moments of silence before you begin.

   - Picture yourself seated across the table from God.

9. Prepare your heart.

   - Observe a few moments of silence in preparation for your time with the Lord.

   - Consider beginning your time with some "nobody's home, belt-it-out" singing!

   - Pray, inviting the Holy Spirit into your time in the Word.

10. Get a new perspective.

Try reading your chosen passage of Scripture from an unfamiliar Bible translation or paraphrase. Wording differences, even subtle ones, require focused attention.

11. Talk to yourself.

We are pretty good at paying attention to ourselves. Combat quiet time distractions by reading Scripture aloud, rephrasing what you read, repeating truths you are learning, or talking through what you are wrestling with.

12. Pray Scripture out loud.

It is much more difficult for your mind to wander off aimlessly when you pray out loud. A marvelous benefit on its own. However, there's another powerful benefit to praying out loud. Satan can hear it. While he does not have the ability to read our minds (1 Kings 8:39), he can hear our spoken words!

13. Combine the spiritual practices.

Fight distraction and reap added benefits to your soul by combining two or more of the spiritual disciplines as you engage with Scripture.

- Combine the discipline of reading the Bible with the discipline of prayer by praying Scripture.

- Read the Bible in solitude or with a soul friend.

- Journal your thoughts as you engage with Scripture.

However you decide to battle the distractions that are guaranteed to come your way, make the fight (Ephesians 6:12) personal.

Begin by making the commitment to fight through the distractions. Add some accountability by writing out your commitment and signing it or sharing it with a friend or family member.

Next, devise your plan. As you craft it, take your unique wiring into consideration. For instance, if you are the type who needs variety, build it into your plan. And above all, give yourself permission to tweak the plan as it's being developed and implemented.

Finally, establish check points for your Distraction Plan. Life seasons change. Our plan may need to change as well. Build automatic review points into your plan, once a year, every six months, quarterly, at the New Year, on your birthday. Then whatever the reason for needed changes, give yourself permission to readjust your plan and keep on going.

God's greatest desire is to spend time with you. He wants to have a relationship with you. He wants you to know Him. The time and effort spent in creating a Distraction Plan are well worth it. Make it a priority. Figure out how to get past the obstacles in order to spend undistracted time with Him.

*"But seek first the kingdom of God and his righteousness,
and all these things will be added to you."* Matthew 6:33

Personal Reflection

1. What are the things that routinely distract you when you sit down with your Bible? Be specific: List each one.

2. With your list from #1 above in mind, go back into the chapter and revisit the Ideas for Creating a Quiet Time Distraction Plan. Make note of any ideas that speak directly to the distractions on your list.

3. Draft your Distraction Plan. To begin, choose no more than three ideas from the list to include in your plan. Don't overwhelm yourself by putting too many items into your plan. Overwhelm often results in total abandonment. Start small. Experience success. Then incorporate additional ideas as you move forward.

4. Finalize your plan. Decide how often and when you will revisit your plan – yearly, every six months, quarterly, etc., and put it on your calendar. Lastly, add this statement to your plan, "I give myself permission to change this plan as needed. I will not beat myself up when my plan does not go as I had hoped. I will, instead, give myself the grace to readjust this plan and to keep on going," and sign it.

5. Pray. Confess your distractions to the Lord and invite Him into your plan.

5

Read It!

Reading the Bible is one of the most basic ways of engaging with God's Word. In Chapter One, we discussed many of the necessities and benefits of Scripture. Let's take a moment to briefly consider three more reasons why it is so important to read the Bible with purpose and intent.

Why Read It?

First, it is vital that we read the Bible because there is a very real battle raging all around us.

> *"For we do not wrestle against flesh and blood, but against the rulers, against the authorities, against the cosmic powers over this present darkness, against the spiritual forces of evil in the heavenly places."* Ephesians 6:12

Sadly, we often go about our days without ever giving this battle a thought. But it is happening. It is real. All around us – a battle for souls!

Satan, the prince of darkness, wants our faith, and He will do all he can to take it. Just look around. Social media, the movies, music, television, advertisements all testify to this fact. Satan is at work. Some of his attacks are blatant, screaming the evils of his plan.

These are the easy ones to spot. Others, however, are subtle, so subtle we are often unaware.

The question is: how do we discern? How are we to know "what is truth" and what is not? The answer is: we find TRUTH in God's Holy Word, and knowing truth requires that we learn to read for meaning.

Please understand that Satan cannot defeat our God. But he can defeat a generation. The battle is real. We must "*fasten on the belt of truth*" (Ephesians 6:14) and take up "*the sword of the Spirit, which is the word of God*" (Ephesians 6:17). Bible reading is our weapon in battle.

Secondly, Bible reading is essential because God speaks to us through His Word. In the book of Hebrews, we read,

> "*Long ago, at many times and in many ways, God spoke to our fathers by the prophets, but in these last days he has spoken to us by his Son, whom he appointed the heir of all things, through whom also he created the world.*" Hebrews 1:1-2

Notice that in verse one of that passage, the author tells us that "*Long ago, at many times and in many ways, God spoke....*" But in verse two he says, "*In these last days he has spoken to us by his Son....*"

"*In these last days,*" is today! Today, God is speaking to us through Jesus. God used to speak "*at many times and in many ways,*" but today, He speaks through His Son, Jesus Christ, through His Spirit in the words of the Bible.

Thirdly, God wants a relationship with us. God wants a relationship with you. Reading the Bible at a deeper level than mere word call is critical because God loves you. In fact, God loves you so much that He gave His only Son for you:

> "*For God so loved the world, that he gave his only Son, that whoever believes in him should not perish but have eternal life.*" John 3:16

Because God loves you, He has a plan for you:

> *"And this is eternal life, that they know you, the only true God, and Jesus Christ whom you have sent."* John 17:3

God loves you so very much that He created you to crave Him. Craving God is the fundamental aim of our life. God's love and His plan are found throughout the Bible. In it we read God's greatest command, love Him:

> *"You shall love the Lord your God with all your heart and with all your soul and with all your mind."* Matthew 22:37

We learn that God "is a jealous God" (Exodus 34:14), jealous for His glory and jealous for us! We see that He says, when we draw near to Him:

> *"He will draw near to [us]."* James 4:8

Since Bible reading is so vitally important, how do we go about reading it in a way that helps us derive meaning from its text?

Read The Bible Skillfully

Let's begin by considering a young child who is just learning to read. Generally, the first thing this emerging reader is taught are the fundamentals of reading. Time is given to the basics such as phonics, letter blends, and how to properly observe punctuation marks. As these are mastered, the budding reader moves on to things like comprehension and reading with inflection.

However, the teaching doesn't stop there. As this young reader progresses, they are schooled in another important aspect of reading. They are taught that there are, in fact, different ways to read. A reader can engage in pleasure reading. Curled up in a comfy spot with a favorite blanket or stuffed animal, a reader can get lost in *Harry Potter*, *Anne of Green Gables*, or *Alexander and the Terrible, Horrible, No Good, Very Bad Day* – just for the fun of it.

On the other hand, a reader might find themselves reading as research. Charged with giving a book report or preparing an oral presentation, the reading will look much different than reading for pleasure. In this case, the reader will sit at a table, paper and pencil (or computer) at the ready, making note of subheadings, bolded words, and charts and graphs.

But it doesn't stop there. Reading students are not only taught the difference in reading styles, they are instructed in the very important skill of matching their reading strategy to their purpose.

It is the same with our Bible. There are different ways to read it.

Read the Bible Privately

This is perhaps one of the most common ways of reading the Bible. Alone in the quiet with as little distraction as possible, you and your Heavenly Father enjoying a visit together in the pages of His Word.

Read the Bible Publicly

The Bible was meant to be read. It was also meant to be heard. Public reading of Scripture is one of the most ancient practices of God's people recorded in Scripture. The first place we find it mentioned in the Bible is at the foot of Mount Sinai as Moses read Scripture aloud to the recently rescued children of Israel (Exodus 24).

There are many other examples of public Bible reading in both the Old and New Testaments. In a time when owning personal copies of the Scriptures was rare, we find:

- Ezra reading the law of Moses to the people of Israel (Nehemiah 8)

- Joshua reading out loud to the Israelites when they entered the new land (Joshua 8)

- King Josiah calling Israel back to the observance of the long-forgotten practice (2 Kings 23)

- Paul's letters being read aloud to gatherings of believers (Colossians 4:16)

- Jesus Himself participating in the public reading of Scripture, and His earthly ministry being launched during the practice (Luke 4:17-21).

Public readings of Scripture reminded the people where they came from, who they were, and what they had been called to. It will do the same for us. As we join together in reading and discussing God's Word, we are forced beyond the comfort of our own personally formed and held beliefs.

We are challenged to see the biblical text in new ways and to wrestle with it. The practice pushes us deeper into the narrative of the Bible helping us remember our story and teaching us how to keep living within its unfolding pages.

Reading Scripture publicly shifts the shaping. Rather than us giving our own shape to the Bible, we are shaped as God's people.

Public Bible reading also guards us from distraction and deception. When we read with others, our attention is not so easily diverted by peripheral noises and wandering thoughts. Public reading keeps us focused on the text.

If private Bible reading is our sole practice, it becomes very easy for God's voice to begin to sound like our own. We can tend to hear His voice speaking out of our culture, our personality, and our preferences. Reading the Word of God with others offers protection from self-deception.

The public reading of Scripture offers another rich, redemptive benefit. It wraps us in community. God created us for community not isolation. It is not possible for our faith to be fully realized when we live as isolated individuals. Public reading of God's Word creates a dynamic community of praise, worship, obedience, honor, hope, and grace.

The practice of reading Scripture publicly is not a common one today. For whatever the reason – accessibility and availability of the Bible, our tendency toward privacy and individualism, ease and comfort, -- we are much more inclined to read in private.

As I reflect on this, I realize that the public reading of God's Word is not a regular part of my Bible reading plan. Typically, my public reading has been a pastor occasionally asking the congregation to stand while he reads the sermon text aloud.

I was delighted, however, on a recent family vacation to visit a church where the entire congregation was asked to stand and read the designated passage together aloud. What a blessing and something I intend to make a more prominent part of my Bible reading.

Perhaps these benefits are what the apostle Paul had in mind when he instructed Timothy to devote himself to the public reading of Scripture:

> *"Until I come, devote yourself to the public reading of Scripture, to exhortation, to teaching."* 1 Timothy 4:13

Read the Bible Silently

Probably the most common form of Scripture Engagement is the silent reading of Scripture. The fastest way to take in Scripture, its advantages include ease, privacy, speed, and volume. Silent reading is great for pre-reading overviews and pleasure reading.

Read the Bible Aloud

Another practice found in the Bible, this is apparently what the Ethiopian Eunuch was doing when Philip came across him in Acts 8:30. Reading aloud slows us down. We typically read aloud at about half the speed of silent reading. It is also far more engaging than silent reading as it helps us take in Scripture through both our eyes and ears.

Reading God's Word aloud can take many forms. Like the Ethiopian Eunuch, one can read the Bible aloud in privacy, or they can listen to someone else read it. Listening to another read Scripture aloud provides a vastly different experience. If a reader is well-prepared and gifted, they can bring out rich meaning from the text through such valuable reading skills as voice inflection, rhythm, and intonation.

Another variation on reading the Bible aloud is reading responsively. This practice combines reading aloud with public reading and is probably the most common form of reading Scripture aloud today.

In responsive reading a leader reads a verse and the "group" responds aloud with the next. Variations can even exist in the makeup of the leader and group. How about men and women, adults and children, grandparents and grandchildren, those with glasses and those without? Done with energy and passion, responsive reading helps move the reader from the act of passive listening to one of active participation.

"Blessed is the one who reads aloud the words of this prophecy."
Revelation 1:3

Read the Bible for Pleasure

It is nourishment to the soul when we come to God's Word, not as something to be checked off our list, but simply because we want to. Like the young child curled up with her stuffed giraffe and tattered blanket reading a copy of her favorite mystery book, sit with your Bible. Carve out time to simply sit and read, because you want to. Once you are settled in that comfy spot, choose a favorite portion and let the Words of God wash over you.

Read the Bible with Focus

Pleasure reading is wonderful and beneficial. However, we cannot live spiritually healthy lives on a diet consisting only of pleasure reading. Deeper, focused reading is absolutely necessary to our soul.

Deeper, focused reading is not one-size fits all. For example, formal Bible study is one way to read with focus. And while formal Bible study is ideal, realistically, it doesn't work in every season of our life. For those seasons (or days) when the intensity of formal Bible study isn't practical, we need to be equipped with other ways to read God's Word with focus.

Focused reading of the Bible is best done with smaller passages than we would typically use when reading for pleasure. Rather than reading entire books or even chapters, consider choosing passages of only a few verses in length or even a single verse.

- Set your focus there and slow your reading pace.

- Read with thought – reflect, ask questions, make connections.

- Record your insights and questions in a journal or your Bible.

Doesn't reading the Bible with focus remind you of our young reader reading as research? Focused Scripture reading is a matter of going back to "reading class." The reading skills you learned in elementary school, and practiced every year thereafter until you graduated, are the same skills needed for focused reading.

The only differences now are that there are no grades, and you aren't required to use the skills assigned by your teacher. When you read the Bible with focus, you are free to choose the skills that work best for you and your passage.

Rethinking our Bible reading strategy can pull us out of a rut and fill us with renewed energy for reading God's Word. Remember our young reader who moved beyond phonics and letter blends to a place where he learned that there are different types of reading?

Come to the Bible knowing that there are many ways to read it – privately, publicly, silently, aloud, for pleasure, and with focus (to name a few). Learn to engage with the Scripture by implementing each one as it matches your purpose.

Personal Reflection

1. At the beginning of this chapter we considered three reasons why it is vital that we read the Bible with purpose and intent:

   - A spiritual battle is raging.

   - God speaks to us through His Word.

   - He wants a deep and intimate relationship with us.

   Reflect on what this knowledge means to you.

2. Several ways to read the Bible were presented in this chapter:

   - Read the Bible privately.
   - Read the Bible publicly.
   - Read the Bible silently.
   - Read the Bible aloud.
   - Read the Bible for pleasure.
   - Read the Bible with focus.

   What are your thoughts on the idea that there are several ways to read the Scripture? Are any of these ways of reading the Bible new to you? Which of these ways might you implement this week? Why this one?

3. Take a trip back to "reading class."

   What reading skills do you remember learning in elementary school?

   Which of these could you bring to reading the Bible with focus?

4. Pray. Ask God to renew your energy and passion for Bible reading. Ask the Holy Spirit to open your eyes, your heart, and your mind as you engage with the Scripture through reading.

Resources
for
Focused Reading

Verse Mapping

The idea behind Verse Mapping is that through the process of examining a verse closely, you can make it yours forever. Verse Mapping works best with a single verse of Scripture.

1. Begin by writing your verse out on whatever "canvas" you've chosen – a loose sheet of paper, in a notebook, on an index card, etc.

2. Leave plenty of "white" space around the verse – on the edges, between the lines, and between the words.

3. Map your verse using the Verse Mapping Guide on the following page.

4. At the close of your "Mapping" time or at the end of your day, take another look at the verse. Write out a prayer sharing with God what you have learned.

Variations:

- Extend your time with a verse. Meditate on it an entire week!

- Make it a family affair. Verse Mapping can be done by anyone regardless of their spiritual maturity or age.
- Map the same verse as a small group or family. Then discuss it.

Verse Mapping Guide

Below are ideas and suggestions for mapping a verse. Choose a single idea or combine any number of ideas as you focus your reading on your verse of Scripture.

- Personalize it. Cross out words like "you," "we," "whoever," and "them." Write *your own* name above the crossed out word.

- Highlight words or phrases that jump out at you. Use different colors.

- Read the verse in context by reading around it. Read the entire passage or chapter.

- Read the verse in at least two other Bible translations. Make note on your page of the words or phrases from the other translations that help you understand or apply the verse. (Many Bible translations are easily accessible through apps and internet sites.)

- Find cross references and note anything that brings new meaning. Cross references are verses that contain similar words or phrases. Again, internet Bible help sites and apps can be of assistance.

- Circle a word or two and do a word study.

  o Look up the word in your dictionary and see if the definition gives you any insight.

  o Use a topical index and/or concordance in the back of your Bible to locate other verses where the word appears.

  o Look up synonyms (same meaning) and antonyms (opposite meaning) in a thesaurus, concordance, or online Bible tools site.

- Write out what you are learning.

- Record your thoughts on how you can apply the Scripture in your daily living.

- Close your study time in prayer and write out your prayer on your Map.

Read the Bible with a Pen (or Lots of Pens!)

1. Substitute your name for personal pronouns.

2. Highlight things that "jump out" at you.

3. Look for repeated words, phrases, or ideas.

4. Search for patterns.

5. Look for key words.

6. Look up word definitions and/or synonyms.

7. Connect words.

8. Make a list.

9. Draw a picture.

10. Ask questions.

11. Locate if/then and cause/effect relationships.

12. If there is a "therefore," ask what it's there for.

13. Rephrase the Scripture using your own words.

14. Summarize.

15. Make application to your daily life.

Be careful not to overwhelm yourself. Do NOT try to do all 15. Pick and choose the ideas that best fit your personality and/or the passage you are reading.

Reading 101

This method for focused Bible reading requires six highlighters or pencils of different color and plenty of space for working. (It may also require a quick refresher course on the parts of speech!) Consider pulling your passage up on your computer, printing it out double- or triple-spaced, and working directly on your printout.

- Underline the subject of each sentence once.

- Underline the predicate twice.

- Highlight nouns and pronouns in one color.

- Highlight verbs in a second color.

- Use a third color to highlight all adjectives including articles.

- Highlight adverbs in a fourth color.

- Highlight conjunctions in a fifth color.

- Use the sixth color to highlight prepositions.

- Draw a rectangle around each name.

- Highlight any mention of time in blue.

- Highlight numbers in yellow.

- Draw a line from each pronoun to its corresponding noun.

- In the margins, make note of your observations including patterns, connections, and/or questions.

Scripture Journaling

Scripture Journaling is a way of studying and responding to the Bible with your own words, sketches, stenciling, images, painting, stamping, or other art media.

What You Need:

Journaling Bible
blank journal, art book, or composition book
Pencil
Fine tip black ink pen
Eraser
Optional: colored pencils, colored markers, stickers, stamps and stamp pads, washi tape, water colors, micron pens, scrap paper, baby wipes, any art materials you have on hand

Process:

Step 1:

Gather your materials. Consider turning on some music to listen to as you journal.

Step 2:

Choose a Scripture verse or passage to journal. (Your selection can come from anywhere: a current Bible study, your personal devotions, family Bible reading, sermon notes, song lyrics, an internet search. The possibilities are endless.)

Step 3:

Read your verse thoughtfully. Ponder how you want to journal the verse:

- Using words only.
- Writing out the verse word for word.
- Recording your thoughts about the verse.
- Combining stickers with words.
- Sketching or drawing.
- Using song lyrics.

Step 4:

Date your entry.

Step 5:

Have fun journaling your Scripture. Don't forget to continue meditating on your Scripture as you work.

Keep in mind that there is no right or wrong way to Scripture journal. You simply cannot do it the wrong way! The idea behind Scripture Journaling is NOT that you create great art. In fact, you do not even have to include art. The idea is that you engage with Scripture and connect with God.

Note: If you are working in a Journaling Bible, be careful not to use materials that will bleed through your pages. You can test your materials on a blank page in the back of your Bible.

Practice with Focused Reading

Verse Mapping Practice

Use the Verse Mapping Guide on page 54 to read Psalm 119:105 with focus.

Your word is a lamp

to my feet

and a light to my path.

Psalm 119:105

Read the Bible with a Pen (or Lots of Pens!) Practice

Read *Psalm 19* with focus. Refer to page 55 if needed.

[1] The heavens declare the glory of God,

and the sky above proclaims his handiwork.

[2] Day to day pours out speech,

and night to night reveals knowledge.

[3] There is no speech, nor are there words,

whose voice is not heard.

[4] Their voice goes out through all the earth,

and their words to the end of the world.

In them he has set a tent for the sun,

[5]   which comes out like a bridegroom leaving his chamber,

and, like a strong man, runs its course with joy.

[6] Its rising is from the end of the heavens,

and its circuit to the end of them,

and there is nothing hidden from its heat.

[7] The law of the Lord is perfect,

    reviving the soul;

the testimony of the Lord is sure,

    making wise the simple;

[8] the precepts of the Lord are right,

    rejoicing the heart;

the commandment of the Lord is pure,

    enlightening the eyes;

[9] the fear of the Lord is clean,

    enduring forever;

the rules of the Lord are true,

    and righteous altogether.

[10] More to be desired are they than gold,

    even much fine gold;

sweeter also than honey

    and drippings of the honeycomb.

¹¹ Moreover, by them is your servant warned;

in keeping them there is great reward.

¹² Who can discern his errors?

Declare me innocent from hidden faults.

¹³ Keep back your servant also from presumptuous sins;

let them not have dominion over me!

Then I shall be blameless,

and innocent of great transgression.

¹⁴ Let the words of my mouth and the meditation of my heart

be acceptable in your sight,

O LORD, my rock and my redeemer.

6

Write It!

Writing Scripture: it's all the rage. If you are a Pinterest person, you've probably seen Scripture Writing Plans populating your feed. Blog reader? You've noticed the plethora of blog posts on the subject. Bible study attender? More than likely, you've come across Scripture writing as part of some of the more recently written studies.

Scripture writing is simply the act of writing out word-for-word by hand selected passages of the Bible. You might wonder why anyone would want to do this when copies of the Bible are so easily accessible. And if like me you find writing anything out by hand to be a tedious and laborious task, the question is ringing in your ears all the louder.

So, why? What's the big deal? Why go to the effort of writing Scripture out by hand?

We write Scripture out word-for-word by hand, because it is biblical. John (Revelation 1:9-11), Paul (2 Thessalonians 3:17), Luke (Luke 1:3), Jeremiah (Jeremiah 30:1-2), Joshua (Joshua 24:26), and the Lord God (Exodus 34:1) all wrote out Scripture. Additionally, Ezra and other Old Testament scribes were esteemed for their knowledge of Scripture which was developed through the copying of God's Word.

Another interesting example occurs in Deuteronomy 17:18-20 where it is recorded that God commanded the kings of Israel to personally write out their own copy of the Bible to be read all the days of their lives. This practice established by God for the kings of Israel should be a testament to us of the value and effectiveness of hand writing Scripture.

The instruction to write Scripture was not reserved only for the kings of Israel. Moses issued the instruction when he said,

"You shall write them on the doorposts of your house and on your gates."
Deuteronomy 6:9

Isaiah spoke it as well,

"And now, go, write it before them on a tablet and inscribe it in a book, that it may be for the time to come as a witness forever." Isaiah 30:8

As we engage in the practice of hand writing Bible text, we mirror the example set by these scribes and kings and apostles, and we can gain the same spiritual benefits that they gained.

Another reason for writing Scripture out word-for-word by hand is that the process slows us down. It forces us to slow down the reading process and encourages us to reflectively engage with God's Word. Our slowed reading tunes us in to details and enables us to see things we don't otherwise see. It provides us with more time to think about the text and to dwell on its meaning and application.

Scripture writing is a focusing activity. As we write, our attention is drawn to the words of the Bible. We are better able to concentrate and "see," very often, in fact, seeing things that fly by during reading alone. The process helps with comprehension, and when extended to include circling, drawing, and noting, helps us make connections that are key to meaning. Far too often we fall victim to "quick reads" of the Bible forgetting what we've read within a very short time. Scripture writing helps combat surface level reading as it focuses us on the text of the Bible.

Writing Scripture also involves the mind and helps with retention. It is an aid to memory. Most of us would agree that writing something down helps us to recall that information later on. Moreover, there is actual science that backs up the power and compelling force that writing has on our minds. When we participate in the act of writing, our Reticular Activity System (RAS) is activated. This system is comprised of the cells at the base of the brain that filter all the information that our brain needs to process.

Research from Princeton University shows that students who take notes on paper actually learn and retain more that those who use laptops. The reason is that handwriting engages different paths of your brain, forces you to more fully process your thinking, creates more and better memory cues for later recall, and gives you an edge in understanding and remembering concepts. (And for what it's worth, there is evidence that cursive reaps even more benefit than print!)

This research was conducted in relation to college students. However, it applies to us as well, because we are students of the Word. The act of writing will affect us in the same manner.

It is important to understand that when we write out something, the information from that writing is brought to the forefront of the brain triggering the brain to pay focused attention to what is being written. This results in the physical act of writing being one of the most effective ways to study and retain new information.

The ability to retain information also means that information is more readily available for recall when needed. Rather than allowing our harried and chaotic days to rob us of our time with God and to zap our strength and energy, we can prepare ahead for these days by arming ourselves with God's strength and power and endurance.

Write, if only for five or ten minutes a day. Write. Then when those times of crazy overload come, you will have already created brain pathways for recalling His Words, words which are able to sustain you. And because this is how God has designed our brains, writing out Scripture by hand can also be a great help when memorizing passages of the Bible.

Another benefit of writing Scripture is that we find rest in the process. This may seem counterintuitive because writing requires some focused energy and physical movement from our body. However, when we sit down and pen words on paper, especially powerful passages from the Bible, our mind finds rest.

Jesus says, "Come to me, all who labor and are heavy laden, and I will give you rest" (Matthew 11:28). Just as writing our personal thoughts out on paper can be therapeutic, writing out God's Truth can have a profound effect on our consciousness. When God takes our burdens as we meditate with pen to paper on the Word, our bodies release and relax.

In addition to affording us rest, writing Scripture leads to intimacy with Christ.

"And this is eternal life, that they know you, the only true God,
and Jesus Christ whom you have sent." John 17:3

The fundamental aim of our life is to know God. When we make the intentional choice to take even ten minutes out of our day to write out the Bible passages we're reading, we are saying, "I choose You, God." Our choice declares that our relationship with God is more important than anything on our to-do list or any 'fire' we feel the need to put out. These moments spent writing His Word, move us toward Him.

During our writing time, no matter its length, our brain processes the words we are writing differently than when we simply read them. (Recall that our Reticular Activity System is activated when we write.) The words become sharper in our minds. They become more than just words. They become ways. They become instructions. They give life. Being intimate with Christ, knowing Him, requires us to be present and fully focused on Him. The simple act of writing Scripture allows this to happen.

What's more the act of writing Scripture out by hand nourishes the soul. Your soul has an infinite capacity to need, and one of its needs is to be with God.

Scripture writing time is time with God. And remember that the physical act of writing brings the powerful words of the Bible to the forefront of the brain, greatly amplifying what God has for us. As these words come to the forefront and we mull them over, deeper meaning is revealed. We enjoy more intimate time with God, our relationship is deepened, and our soul finds the nourishment that only time with Him and the truth of His Word can provide.

In his letter to the Philippians, Paul said,

"Finally, brothers, whatever is true, whatever is honorable, whatever is just, whatever is pure, whatever is lovely, whatever is commendable, if there is any excellence, if there is anything worthy of praise, think about these things." Philippians 4:8

Writing Scripture is one way to follow Paul's instruction to think on these things. No, the purpose of writing God's Word out by hand is not so that we can have another copy of it. The ultimate purpose is to know God by engaging with the Bible.

Personal Reflection

1. What were your initial thoughts on the idea of writing Scripture out by hand as a means for engaging with Scripture? What impact, if any, did the Bible evidence of Scripture writing have on your initial opinion?

2. Hand writing Scripture has many benefits, some of which are: slowing down our reading pace, focusing our attention, increasing our retention/recall of information, rest, intimacy with Christ, and nourishment to the soul. Which of these surprises you or speaks to you in your current season?

3. Select a favorite passage of Scripture. First, simply read the passage. Then, write it out by hand. Reflect on your experience by writing out your thoughts and observations.

4. Pray. Ask God what He has for you regarding the writing out of Scripture. Ask Him how you might best begin to incorporate this practice into your time in His Word.

Resources
for
Writing Scripture

Tips for Hand-writing Scripture

- Designate a journal, notebook, or composition book to the purpose of hand-writing the Scripture.

- Prepare a quiet place for your work. Reduce distractions as much as possible and have your materials ready.

- Quiet your mind. Quiet your heart.

- Pray. Ask the Holy Spirit to reveal truth to you and to keep you focused.

- Get the BIG picture. Read through the entire passage from beginning to end BEFORE writing it out. This will help you see the book as a whole which is important to contextual understanding.

- Write. Slowly, thoughtfully. Focus on each word as you write it out. Ask what it means in both the immediate and the broader context.

Do not rush the process. The goal is not to have another copy of God's Word. The goal is to engage with Scripture and in so doing, to meet with God.

Verse a Day Scripture Writing

- Create a place for recording your handwritten Scripture. Think about your daily habits and personality. If you are the daily planner sort, write your verse directly into your planner. Another option is to set up a journal dedicated to this purpose.

- Be on the lookout for verses to write out each day. Verses can come from anywhere: a current Bible study, your Pastor's Sunday sermon, Bible apps, your list of favorites.

- Read through the verse a time or two before setting about to write it out.

- Write the entire verse in cursive lettering. (Optional: Print the verse, using cursive for words you wish to emphasize.)

- Think about each word as you write.

Variation:

As an aid to Scripture meditation and/or memorization, write out the selected verse several days in a row. Few things are more helpful than repetition. Writing out the same Scripture multiple times can help you internalize it. Write slowly, thinking about each word as you write.

Scripture Writing Plans

- Do an internet search for "Scripture Writing Plans."

- Look through the results keeping an eye out for topics and books of the Bible that are of interest to you.

- Select a plan.

- In a journal, notebook, or composition book, write out by hand each day's Scripture.

- Date your entries daily.

- From time to time consider writing out a reflection on the process and/or what you are learning.

Journible-Style Scripture Writing

This method of Scripture writing is especially suited to longer passages of the Bible such as entire books.

- Select the passage you would like to write out.

- Get the big picture. Read completely through the passage at least once before beginning the writing process.

- Choose a journal or notebook to work in. (Composition books are a great choice for this style of Scripture writing. They contain plenty of pages and are inexpensive.)

- Write your selected passage of the Bible on the right-hand pages of your book. As you write skip one or two lines between the lines of text.

- In this style of Scripture writing, the left-hand page is left open for use in engaging even more deeply with the text. Write your thoughts, reflections, observations, questions about the text on the right-hand page on the corresponding left-hand page. Consider including:

  o Observations from the text: patterns, connections, etc.

  o Definitions, synonyms, antonyms.

  o What you are learning about God from the text.

  o What the passage is teaching you about yourself.

  o How what you are learning can be applied to daily life.

  o Any questions you may have.

  o Prayers.

Make Journible-Style Scripture Writing fit you.

Option 1:

Write out the entire book/passage first. Then interact with the text after it has been written out.

Option 2:

Write out the Scripture and interact with it in intervals. For example, write out one chapter at a time reflecting on each before moving on to the next.

Option 3:

Any writing/interacting plan that works best for you.

"Write and Code" Scripture Writing Plan

This Scripture Writing method is best suited to passages of multiple verses such as chapters, sermons, or prayers.

- First, read complete through your passage from beginning to end.

- Hand copy your passage onto your page or into your journal. (Remember: Cursive is even more beneficial than print!)

- Optional: Make any words that seem to jump out at you stand out on your page by writing them in all caps or with creative lettering.

- When finished go back into your handwritten passage and read it with focus.

    o Circle repeated words, phrases, or ideas.

    o Make note of any patterns you notice.

    o Draw arrows between related thoughts.

    o Write out an application.

Practice
with
Writing Scripture

Scripture Writing Practice

On the lines below hand-write Deuteronomy 6:4-9.

1. Read through the passage before putting pen to page.

2. Remember: Cursive is even more beneficial than print.

3. Make any words that seem to jump out at you stand out on your page by writing them in ALL CAPS or with creative lettering.

4. If time permits, go back and read your hand-written passage with focus. Circle repeated words, phrases, or ideas; make note of any visible patterns; draw arrows between related thoughts; and/or write out an application.

_____

_____

_____

_____

_____

_____

_____

_____

_____

_____

_____

_____

_____

_____

7

Meditate on It!

A couple of years ago I wrote a blog post about a method of Scripture meditation. That post nearly went unpublished. Just days before the post was scheduled to be released, I simply had to check some things – one more time. I sat at my computer, plugged in my search terms, and this time the results returned were totally negative. Solid Christian leaders who I trusted were absolutely opposed to this method of meditation. Completely baffled, I began to question myself. Was something lacking in my research? Had I not been thorough? Was I blinded to the truth? Had I swallowed subtle lies?

As the day went on, I concluded that it would be safer not to share the post. It would not be missed. After all, no one even knew it had been my plan, and I could not risk sharing something that was not biblically sound. Unable, however, to let it go, I recounted my plight with my husband at dinner that evening. He listened, and then very wisely reminded me of the Pharisees and how they were often cited in the Bible for taking good things and twisting them to fit their purposes. He ended by pointing out that there will always be people who twist what God intended for good.

This is why I love the following quote about Biblical meditation.

"One hindrance to growth among Christians today is our failure to cultivate spiritual knowledge. We fail to give enough time to prayer and Bible-reading, and we have abandoned the practice of meditation. How tragic that the very word meditation, once regarded as a core discipline of Christianity and 'a crucial preparation for and adjunct to the work of prayer,' is now associated with unbiblical 'New Age' spirituality." Dr. Joel R. Beeke [1]

Biblical Meditation is the act of carefully considering a passage of Scripture in its original context, mulling over its full meaning, and evaluating its application to our own life. It is an active process. The spiritual discipline of Biblical Meditation is NOT the meditation of Eastern Mysticism. Eastern Mystic (New Age) meditation calls for an emptying of the mind. Biblical Meditation is, in fact, the complete opposite of the meditation of Eastern Mysticism. Meditating biblically requires the filling of your mind with a verse or passage and letting it soak in deeply. It is what God instructs us to do… set your mind on, think on, fill your mind.

Today, we have largely lost the puritan art of meditation spoken of by Dr. Beeke. The Puritans practiced two types of spiritual meditation, occasional and deliberate.

Occasional Meditation is brief meditation that takes place in the hustle and bustle of daily life. In this type of meditation, one takes what is observed with the senses and raises it up to God in thought. Occasional Meditation is a complement to praying without ceasing. The Puritan people were encouraged to see all the world around them as a stage for seeing God's wisdom and glory, just as David did with the moon and stars (Psalm 8:3-4), Solomon did with the ant (Prov. 6:6-8) and our Lord taught us by the lilies of the field (Matt. 6:28-30) and the water from the well (John 4:7-15). Occasional meditation can be practiced any time, any place, by anyone.

Deliberate Meditation was a time for Puritans to spend in focused thinking upon Scripture. It was practiced during set periods of time, especially in the morning, evening, and on the Sabbath. This is the meditation we refer to when we talk about engaging with the Scripture.

To meditate on God's Word, we first acquaint ourselves with the text by reading and rereading it. Most helpful is to read it aloud, which helps with focus, listening, and truly hearing the text. We then linger long with the text of our passage by reading it again and again; noticing words, phrases, and ideas; reflecting; asking questions; and interacting with the passage in ways that affect our heart and inform our mind.

"What value is there to reading one, three, or more chapters of Scripture only to find that after you've finished, you can't recall a thing you've read? It's better to read a small amount of Scripture and meditate on it than to read an extensive section without meditation." Donald S. Whitney [2]

Personal Reflection

1. Reflect on the verse below based on our definition of biblical meditation.

   "This Book of the Law shall not depart from your mouth, but you shall meditate on it day and night, so that you may be careful to do according to all that is written in it. For then you will make your way prosperous, and then you will have good success." Joshua 1:8

2. To meditate on a passage of Scripture is to linger long with it. How would you go about immersing yourself in Joshua 1:8, allowing it to affect your heart and inform your mind?

3. Pray. Ask the Lord to incline your heart to His Word and to help you know Him.

Resources
for
Meditating on Scripture

22 Benefits of Meditating on Scripture *

1. Meditation helps us focus on the Triune God, to love and to enjoy Him in all His persons (1 John 4:8)—intellectually, spiritually, aesthetically.

2. Meditation helps increase knowledge of sacred truth. It "takes the veil from the face of truth" (Prov. 4:2).

3. Meditation is the "nurse of wisdom," for it promotes the fear of God, which is the beginning of wisdom (Prov. 1:8).

4. Meditation enlarges our faith by helping us to trust the God of promises in all our spiritual troubles and the God of providence in all our outward troubles.

5. Meditation augments one's affections. Watson called meditation "the bellows of the affections." He said, "Meditation hatcheth good affections, as the hen her young ones by sitting on them; we light affection at this fire of meditation" (Ps. 39:3).

6. Meditation fosters repentance and reformation of life (Ps. 119:59; Ez. 36:31).

7. Meditation is a great friend to memory.

8. Meditation helps us view worship as a discipline to be cultivated. It makes us prefer God's house to our own.

9. Meditation transfuses Scripture through the texture of the soul.

10. Meditation is a great aid to prayer (Ps. 5:1). It tunes the instrument of prayer before prayer.

11. Meditation helps us to hear and read the Word with real benefit. It makes the Word "full of life and energy to our souls." William Bates wrote, "Hearing the word is like ingestion, and when we meditate upon the word that is digestion; and this digestion of the word by meditation produceth warm affections, zealous resolutions, and holy actions."

12. Meditation on the sacraments helps our "graces to be better and stronger." It helps faith, hope, love, humility, and numerous spiritual comforts thrive in the soul.

13. Meditation stresses the heinousness of sin. It "musters up all weapons and gathers all forces of arguments for to presse our sins, and lay them heavy upon the heart," wrote Fenner. Thomas Hooker said, "Meditation sharpens the sting and strength of corruption, that it pierceth more prevailingly." It is a "strong antidote against sin" and "a cure of covetousness."

14. Meditation enables us to "discharge religious duties, because it conveys to the soul the lively sense and feeling of God's goodness; so the soul is encouraged to duty."

15. Meditation helps prevent vain and sinful thoughts (Jer. 4:14; Matt. 12:35). It helps wean us from this present evil age.

16. Meditation provides inner resources on which to draw (Ps. 77:10-12), including direction for daily life (Prov. 6:21-22).

17. Meditation helps us persevere in faith; it keeps our hearts "savoury and spiritual in the midst of all our outward and worldly employments," wrote William Bridge.

18. Meditation is a mighty weapon to ward off Satan and temptation (Ps. 119:11,15; 1 John 2:14).

19. Meditation provides relief in afflictions (Is. 49:15-17; Heb. 12:5).

20. Meditation helps us benefit others with our spiritual fellowship and counsel (Ps. 66:16; 77:12; 145:7).

21. Meditation promotes gratitude for all the blessings showered upon us by God through His Son.

22. Meditation glorifies God (Ps. 49:3).[3]

*From "The Puritan Practice of Meditation" by Dr. Joel R. Beeke

How to Meditate on God's Word

A Few Ideas:

- Read, read, and reread.

- Read it out loud – several times.

- Think about each word as you read the passage aloud. Let the words roll around in your mind.

- Read it several times, putting the emphasis on a different word each time.

- Read with a friend.

- Using a Bible app, listen to the passage over-and-over again.

- Read with a pen (or a set of color pencils) – personalize, highlight, color code, circle, draw lines.

- Mark the different parts of speech.

- Make lists – characteristics, commands, promises, insights, etc.

- Find connections.

- Verse Map.

- Write it out by hand.

- Rewrite a verse or passage in your own words.

- Summarize it.

- Do a word-study.

- Put yourself in the passage. What do you notice? What emotions do you feel?

- Look for Christ. How does the passage point to Him?

- Ask, "What does this passage teach me about God?"

- Pray the Scriptures.

Lectio Divina (literally "Sacred Reading")

Lectio Divina is a traditional method of Scripture meditation. The process of Bible reading and prayer encourage communion with God. As a spiritual practice, Lectio Divina is a vehicle for filling your mind with a verse, passage, or truth of God and letting it soak in deeply.

Lectio (reading):

- Read through the entire passage very slowly. Take the time to note every word.

- Think about the order of the words.

- Look for patterns, repetitions, themes, images, and dialogue.

- Place yourself inside the scene.

- Watch for a single word, phrase, verse, metaphor, or message that catches your eye, stirs you, moves you, or connects with you emotionally.

- Read through the passage again. What is jumping out at you? Read that portion multiple times. Read it out loud. Linger there.

- Imagine that the author is speaking the words to you. Think about his tone.

- Feel the words with your heart and soul. Allow them to inform your mind.

Meditatio (meditation):

Fill your mind with God's Word. Let it soak in deeply.

- Continue reading and rereading the passage.
- Notice the grammatical structure of the passage.
- Write it out by hand.
- Listen to it over and over.
- Find connections.
- Rewrite it in your own words.

- Ask questions.
  - How does this passage fit into the Bible narrative?
  - What does it teach me about God?
  - How can I apply this to my daily life?
- Ask the Holy Spirit to open your eyes and mind to the passage.

Caution: Take care to guard against inventing biblical meaning for yourself. The purpose here is not to make things up about the Bible but to commune with God and to know Him.

Oratio (prayer):

Take all the thoughts, feelings, actions, fears, convictions, and questions you have meditated on and offer them to the Lord in prayer.

- Praise God for who He is.
- If confession is necessary, offer it.
- Ask for guidance on taking any needed next steps.
- If you feel thankful for something that God has done for you, express sincere gratitude.
- Present your anxieties, worries, and fears to God.
- Pray for the guidance and peace to be able to submit to God's will.

Contemplatio (contemplation):

- Be silent in the presence of God (Psalm 46:10).
- Relax.
- Don't talk.
- Sit. Feel His embrace. Experience His love.
- As you close, commit yourself to God's truth. Submit to His Word.
- Offer a prayer of thanksgiving.

Stress the Word

This method of Scripture meditation is best suited to a single verse or phrase.

1. Read your passage several times, preferably out loud.

2. Each time you read it, stress a different word.

Example: Psalm 63:1

O God, you are my God; earnestly I seek you; my soul thirsts for you; my flesh faints for you...

O **God**, you are my God; earnestly I seek you; my soul thirsts for you; my flesh faints for you...

O God, **you** are my God; earnestly I seek you; my soul thirsts for you; my flesh faints for you...

O God, you **are** my God; earnestly I seek you; my soul thirsts for you; my flesh faints for you...

O God, you are **my** God; earnestly I seek you; my soul thirsts for you; my flesh faints for you...

O God, you are my **God**; earnestly I seek you; my soul thirsts for you; my flesh faints for you...

Continue until each word of the passage has been stressed.

Bold = *stressed word*

Practice with Meditating on Scripture

Meditating on Scripture Practice

Biblical Meditation – the act of carefully considering a passage of Scripture in its original context, mulling over its full meaning, and evaluating its application to our own life. It is an active process.

1. Read through Dr. Beeke's "22 Benefits of Meditating on Scripture" (page 89) and choose one that speaks to you.

2. Look up the corresponding verse and write it out by hand.

3. Select 1-3 ideas from "How to Meditate on God's Word" (page 91) and use them to meditate upon your chosen scripture.

Benefit of Meditating on Scripture # _____

Corresponding Scripture verse: _____

_____

_____

_____

_____

_____

_____

_____

_____

_____

_____

8

Memorize It!

Memorizing Scripture is one of the most effective ways to engage with Scripture. Because Scripture engagement is about interacting with the Bible text which involves such things as reflecting on and mulling over passages, memorized Scriptures make the process available to us 24/7. Having portions of Bible text memorized means we can dwell continuously on them.

In an age when Bibles are so easily accessible, putting forth the effort to memorize Scripture might seem unnecessary. After all, memorization is work, hard work. And for most of us the memorization muscles have atrophied. We don't memorize much of anything, let alone portions of the Bible. However, there are several critically important reasons for memorizing Scripture.

First, as we've already alluded to, memorizing Scripture is one of the most effective ways to mediate upon it. The process of memorizing necessarily requires that we spend time with and think on what we are memorizing. In other words, memorization involves meditation. Reciprocally, once the passage has been committed to our memory, it is always available to us for meditation.

Scripture that has been memorized also helps us to guard against sin. Memorized passages are always with us and available for recall. This is particularly helpful when we are being tempted. Psalm 119:11 is clear about this relationship between memorized Scripture and the power to resist temptation. And Matthew 4:1-11 confirms the relationship as Jesus quotes memorized Scripture to combat the temptations of Satan.

Another reason to memorize portions of the Bible is that it helps us grow to be more like Jesus. As we use memorized passages to share our faith with those who don't yet have a personal relationship with Christ, offer blessings of encouragement to our hurting sisters and brothers, and speak words of admonition to those who are struggling, we grow in grace and knowledge of Jesus Christ.

"But grow in the grace and knowledge of our Lord and Savior Jesus Christ. To him be the glory both now and to the day of eternity. Amen." 2 Peter 3:18

Spiritual Food

It is important that we keep in mind that the Words of the Bible are our spiritual food. The Bible, in fact, is often referred to as food. It is called milk in 1 Peter 2:2, water in John 4:14, bread in John 6:35, and meat in Hebrews 5:12-14, KJV.

It is a fact that the physical food we take into our physical body does not nourish us unless we properly digest it and take it into our cells. Just as physical food is needed for physical strength, spiritual food is necessary for spiritual strength. The Word you read (the spiritual food) must be chewed, digested, and taken into your being, and one way to chew your food is by memorization.

But I can't! It's too hard. I'm too old. My brain is too full. I simply cannot memorize! We are all full of reasons why we think we can't memorize Scripture, but I might insert here that I know that I am perfectly capable of memorizing the things I want to memorize. For example, I have absolutely no trouble memorizing song lyrics. Don't let those negative thoughts rob you of the joy and benefits of this powerful Scripture engagement practice.

Memorization was a prevalent practice in Bible times. Examples of it are strewn throughout the text, and it is clear Jesus, himself, memorized Scripture. The practice helped those in Bible times to live faithful lives and grow to be more like Christ. It will help us, too, and it is actually fun.

"Bible memorization is absolutely fundamental to spiritual formation. If I had to choose between all the disciplines of the spiritual life, I would choose Bible memorization, because it is a fundamental way of filling our minds with what it needs. This book of the law shall not depart out of your mouth. That's where you need it! How does it get in your mouth? Memorization." Dallas Willard [1]

Personal Reflection

1. What is typically your first reaction to the thought of memorizing Scripture? List any excuses you may have used in the past for not attempting Scripture memorization.

2. Are there things you do memorize easily? What are they? (Song lyrics, passwords, quirky sayings, jokes, etc.)

3. Think through some of the benefits of having Scripture committed to memory. Which are most important to you?

4. Pray. If you are feeling a push-back when it comes to Scripture memorization, ask God to incline your heart toward the practice. Then try memorizing just one verse.

Resources
for
Memorizing Scripture

Tips for Memorizing Scripture

- Hand write the Scripture you want to memorize.

  The physical act of writing is good for your brain and aids in retention.

- Say it out loud.

  "Saying a verse one hundred times in one day is not as helpful as saying it every day for one hundred days. The absolute key to successful Scripture memorization is repetition over a long time period." Dr. Andrew Davis [2]

- Review, review, review… and review some more!

  Begin each day's memorization session with a review of previously memorized passages.

- Meditate on your Scripture.

  Word by word. Soak it in!

- Pray it.

- Sing it.

  Search the internet for a Scripture song of your passage or give it your own tune.

- Photograph it.

  With your mind. Or literally. Take a picture of your Scripture and post it in a visible spot.

  BONUS IDEA: Make the passage your screen saver.

• Have your Bible nearby each time you review.

When you just "can't remember," look. It doesn't hurt. In fact, it will probably help in the long run.

• Memorize the verse numbers.

When memorizing longer passages, include the verse number as if it were part of your verse. This practice will help you keep from dropping verses or phrases as you recite passages. It will also help you identify and pull out individual verses.

• Add feeling and interpretation as you recite your verses.

This practice is a form of meditation and helps with internalization and recall.

• Ask a friend to listen as you recite a verse you are working on.

• Memorize with others, one friend or a group.

A Method for Memorizing Verses

Step One:

Read, Read, Read. Read your verse in context. Read the surrounding Scripture text. Read the verse in other translations. Read paraphrases of the verse. Read what others have written about the verse.

Step Two:

Read the verse itself several times. Read it out loud. Pay attention to each word on the page as you read.

Step Three:

Close your Bible and recite the verse eight to ten times.

Step Four:

The next day, open your Bible and read the verse again in order to refresh your memory. Close your Bible and recite the verse eight to ten times. Repeat this step daily until you feel that you have the verse memorized.

Step Five:

With the verse committed to memory, choose a new verse and begin the process again.

Review:

As you work to memorize new verses, don't forget to REVIEW the old ones. Repeat newly memorized Scriptures often, daily, over many days.

A Method for Memorizing Longer Passages of Scripture

First Day:

Read the first verse of your chosen passage out loud ten times. Read it word for word. Look at each word on the page as you read.

After you have read the verse ten times, recite it ten times. Close your Bible or exit your app and say the verse ten times without looking.

Second Day:

Recite the previous day's verse ten times. If you need to, refresh your memory first by opening your Bible and reading the verse.

Now, move to the new verse. Read the next verse in your selected passage. Just as you did on Day One, read it carefully, word for word, out loud ten times. When finished, cover the verse and recite it ten times.

Third Day:

Recite the previous day's verse ten times. Refresh your memory first if needed.

Next, recite the verses from all previous days together, verse one followed by verse two. Do this at least once. In the early days when the groupings of verses are short, it's a good idea to repeat this step multiple times.

Add the new verse. Read it out loud ten times. See each word as you read. Without looking, recite the verse ten times.

You're done for the day.

Continue with this same pattern until you have memorized an entire chapter or book of the Bible.

Pattern Day One:

Read the day's verse ten times, out loud, giving attention to each word as you read.

Without looking, recite the verse ten times.

Pattern All Other Days:

Recite the previous day's verse ten times. Refresh your memory first if needed.

As a whole, recite all previous verses from the passages.

Read the day's new verse ten times, out loud, giving attention to each word as it is read.

Without looking, recite the verse ten times.

Practice
with
Memorizing Scripture

Memorizing Scripture Practice

Choose at least 3 ideas from "Tips for Memorizing Scripture" on page 105 to help you memorize *Psalm 100*.

Psalm 100

[1] Make a joyful noise to the Lord, all the earth!

[2] Serve the Lord with gladness!

 Come into his presence with singing!

[3] Know that the Lord, he is God!

It is he who made us, and we are his;

we are his people, and the sheep of his pasture.

[4] Enter his gates with thanksgiving,

and his courts with praise!

Give thanks to him; bless his name!

[5] For the Lord is good;

his steadfast love endures forever,

and his faithfulness to all generations.

9

Pray It!

According to Evan Howard, in his book *Praying the Scriptures*, "To pray the Scriptures is to order one's time of prayer around a particular text in the Bible." [1]

An incredible way to engage with God's Word, Praying Scripture calls us to a posture of thoughtful reading as we speak to God in natural response to the Bible text. Using words, phrases, and ideas from the text we fashion a prayer of response.

Often the time we spend with God is one of singular focus. We sit with Him as we read our Bible. We talk with Him in prayer. Sometimes we read our Bible and then close out our time in prayer, but even then, we are engaging in each of the disciplines separately. Praying Scripture is not reading and then praying. It is prayerful reading, and it is powerful.

One of the marvelous things about praying Scripture is that it helps strengthen "prayer" confidence. Many of us struggle with what to pray or whether we are praying "correctly." Others fall into ruts of dullness or repetition. When we pray the words of the Bible, we never have to question if our prayers are "right." And using the words and emotions of the Bible text will remedy dullness, repetition, and knowing what to pray.

Scripture prayers can take many forms. For instance, we can pray the text word-for-word, personalize passages, or pray through topics of the Bible. There is no set formula for choosing which form our Scripture prayers should take. Rather, our choice should be made as we read, thoughtfully guided by the Holy Spirit. Additionally, the words, language structure, and tone of our prayer should naturally reflect that of the text.

One way to pray Scripture is to pray its very words. The Bible is full of prayers. For those just starting out on this journey, you might want to begin with any of the Psalms or the prayers of Paul in the New Testament. Sit with your Bible. Quiet your mind. Then slowly, thoughtfully read through the prayer. As you read each word, contemplate, reflect, make it your own.

Praying the prayers of the Bible helps us identify with their authors and the emotions and experiences that were a very real part of their lives. It allows us to freely express our own emotions while showing us that doing so is not wrong. The practice of praying Scripture word-for-word also teaches us how to pray and strengthens our spiritual lives.

Another way to pray Scripture is to personalize the passages as they are read, and there are many, many ways to personalize them. One of my favorite ways is to replace any pronouns in the text with your own name as you read/pray the Scripture back to God. Other ways to personalize passages as you pray Scripture are to claim any promises as your own, ask the Holy Spirit to help you obey any commands, or profess a need as your own. Additionally, if a verse or passage states God's design for our lives, ask Him to help you live according to His design.

While the prayers of the Bible are ideal for the discipline of praying Scripture, we are not limited to these "prayer" passages. Any portion of Scripture can be prayed. As we read other portions of Bible text thoughtfully, in His presence, we will find that they inspire powerful prayers. Begin by inviting the Holy Spirit into your prayer reading. Then pay attention. The Bible is God's Word to us. It reveals, tells, declares, and identifies God. And each of these offers opportunity for us to respond in praise, thanksgiving, heartfelt plea, or confession.

Another way to pray Scripture is by topic. There may be times in your life when you are faced with a specific need or find yourself emotionally stretched. At other times you may have the desire to be encouraged, give thanks, or offer confession. Whatever your need, you might be blessed by locating passages on the topic at hand and praying them.

Praying Scripture is a powerful discipline and one of great value to any believer in Christ, no matter their age or level of spiritual maturity. When we pray Scripture, we know we are praying truth and praying according to God's will. Additionally, it is a mighty weapon against Satan and his attacks. If this way of engaging the Scripture is new to you, helpful resources for getting started are available at the end of this chapter. There is simply nothing quite like spending time with the Lord as we pray His very God-breathed words. It helps us grow deeper in relationship with Him and places our focus squarely where it needs to be.

Personal Reflection

1. Go back and reread Evan Howard's definition of Praying Scripture. Then skim over the ideas presented in this chapter for engaging in the discipline. In your own words, what does it mean to pray Scripture?

2. Which of the ways to pray Scripture speaks to you today?

3. Think about your favorite passages of Scripture. Jot a couple of them down. Have you ever considered praying them?

4. Pray. Choose one of the favorite passages from your list in #3 above and pray it any way you like – word-for-word, inserting your name and making it personal, or in response to what God is saying to you.

Resources
for
Praying Scripture

TIPS for Praying Scripture

- Designate a place and eliminate distractions as much as possible.

- Before you begin, quiet your mind and invite the Holy Spirit into your time.

- Pray the meaning of the passage not just the words.

- Pray thoughtfully – contemplate, meditate, reflect.

- Read the passage in context.

- Search out who wrote the passage, the audience, the culture, etc.

- Write out your prayers, include the date.

- Write out the Scriptures by hand. Post them in visible areas or carry them with you and read them as prayers.

- Create a Scripture Prayer Journal. Section your journal off by topic – prayers for family, prayers for personal growth, prayers for comfort, prayers of praise, etc. Collect Scriptures to pray by writing them in the appropriate section of your journal. Pull out your journal when you feel the need for prayer in a certain area.

Pray the Psalms

A tried-and-true method: Select a numbered Psalm that corresponds to the current day of the month.

Day 1   Psalm 1, Psalm 31, Psalm 61, Psalm 91, or Psalm 121

Day 2   Psalm 2, Psalm 32, Psalm 62, Psalm 92, or Psalm 122

Day 3   Psalm 3, Psalm 33, Psalm 63, Psalm 93, or Psalm 123

Day 4   Psalm 4, Psalm 34, Psalm 64, Psalm 94, or Psalm 124

Day 5   Psalm 5, Psalm 35, Psalm 65, Psalm 95, or Psalm 125

Day 6   Psalm 6, Psalm 36, Psalm 66, Psalm 96, or Psalm 126

Day 7   Psalm 7, Psalm 37, Psalm 67, Psalm 97, or Psalm 127

Day 8   Psalm 8, Psalm 38, Psalm 68, Psalm 98, or Psalm 128

Day 9   Psalm 9, Psalm 39, Psalm 69, Psalm 99, or Psalm 129

Day 10   Psalm 10, Psalm 40, Psalm 70, Psalm 100, or Psalm 130

Day 11   Psalm 11, Psalm 41, Psalm 71, Psalm 101, or Psalm 131

Day 12   Psalm 12, Psalm 42, Psalm 72, Psalm 102, or Psalm 132

Day 13   Psalm 13, Psalm 43, Psalm 73, Psalm 103, or Psalm 133

Day 14   Psalm 14, Psalm 44, Psalm 74, Psalm 104, or Psalm 134

Day 15   Psalm 15, Psalm 45, Psalm 75, Psalm 105, or Psalm 135

Day 16   Psalm 16, Psalm 46, Psalm 76, Psalm 106, or Psalm 136

Day 17	Psalm 17, Psalm 47, Psalm 77, Psalm 107, or Psalm 137
Day 18	Psalm 18, Psalm 48, Psalm 78, Psalm 108, or Psalm 138
Day 19	Psalm 19, Psalm 49, Psalm 79, Psalm 109, or Psalm 139
Day 20	Psalm 20, Psalm 50, Psalm 80, Psalm 110, or Psalm 140
Day 21	Psalm 21, Psalm 51, Psalm 81, Psalm 111, or Psalm 141
Day 22	Psalm 22, Psalm 52, Psalm 82, Psalm 112, or Psalm 142
Day 23	Psalm 23, Psalm 53, Psalm 83, Psalm 113, or Psalm 143
Day 24	Psalm 24, Psalm 54, Psalm 84, Psalm 114, or Psalm 144
Day 25	Psalm 25, Psalm 55, Psalm 85, Psalm 115, or Psalm 145
Day 26	Psalm 26, Psalm 56, Psalm 86, Psalm 116, or Psalm 146
Day 27	Psalm 27, Psalm 57, Psalm 87, Psalm 117, or Psalm 147
Day 28	Psalm 28, Psalm 58, Psalm 88, Psalm 118, or Psalm 148
Day 29	Psalm 29, Psalm 59, Psalm 89, Psalm 119, or Psalm 149
Day 30	Psalm 30, Psalm 60, Psalm 90, Psalm 120, or Psalm 150
Day 31	Choose any Psalm or read Psalm 119

Remember: Praying Scripture is all about engaging with the Bible and conversing with your Heavenly Father. Don't overwhelm yourself by taking on too much. Rather than trying to pray through all five chapters each day, choose one, any one, and spend your time there.

Praying Scripture in Color [2]

Select a single verse or short passage of Scripture. Then use one of the following options to pray the verse in color.

Option 1:

Write your chosen verse of Scripture on a sheet of paper or on your journal page. Meditate on the verse by reading it over and over, either aloud or in your head. Talk with God about what the verse means. As you spend time with the Scripture and with God, keep your pencil moving by adding color and design to your page.

Option 2:

Write out your Scripture verse. Spend some time quietly reading over the verse several times. Ask God to give you a word or a phrase. Then circle the word/phrase that jumps out at you. (If nothing jumps out, simply choose.) Next, concentrate your meditation, prayer, color, and design on that word/phrase. What is God revealing to you about how that word relates to other words in the passage? What is He revealing to you about His character? What truth is being uncovered?

Option 3:

After reading over your Scripture verse, draw out a design on a sheet of paper or in your journal. Go back to your verse. As you meditate on the verse, add its words and your thoughts, reflections, or questions to the design you drew.

Practice with Praying Scripture

Praying Scripture Practice #1

Select a passage of Scripture to pray. If you are not sure where to begin, choose one from the list below.

Quiet your mind and invite the Holy Spirit into your prayer.

Read thoughtfully, one word at a time. Contemplate, meditate, reflect. Pray the meaning of the passage not just the words.

- Psalm 23
- Psalm 42:1-5
- Psalm 63
- Psalm 84:10-12
- Psalm 100
- Matthew 6:9-13

- Romans 5:1-11
- Ephesians 1:15-23
- Ephesians 3:14-21
- Philippians 1:9-11
- Colossians 1:3-1

Praying Scripture Practice #2

- Psalm 23
- Psalm 42:1-5
- Psalm 63
- Psalm 84:10-12

- Psalm 100
- Matthew 6:9-13
- Romans 5:1-11
- Ephesians 1:15-23

- Ephesians 3:14-21
- Philippians 1:9-11
- Colossians 1:3-1

1. Choose one of the Scripture passages above.

2. By hand, write the passage out in prayer form.

- Personalize it by inserting your name for any pronouns.

- Respond:

  o What are you are learning about God through the passage?

  o Give praise and offer thanksgiving for who He is and what He has done.

  o How does the passage apply to you? Write out an application for daily living.

10

Interwoven

Read It, Write It, Meditate on It, Memorize It, and Pray It – each one is a powerful and valuable way to engage with Scripture. But did you notice how easily and naturally they intertwine?

We know that the spiritual disciplines such as Bible reading, prayer, solitude, and self-reflection, perform their best work in our souls when they are interwoven with one another. It is the same with these methods for engaging with Scripture – they perform their best work in our souls when they are interwoven one with another.

For example, writing out Scripture by hand reaps a multitude of benefits and is well worth doing as a solitary practice. However, it also fits beautifully with meditating on Scripture, memorizing it, and praying it. The physical act of writing that we discovered helps slow us down, focus, and pay attention to the text, is a natural fit with all the other methods of Scripture engagement.

Truly, the pairings are many. Meditate by reading with focus. Write out the Scripture you are committing to memory. As you pray Scripture, meditate. Memorize the verses you are meditating on. How about meditating on a passage by reading it with focus and then memorizing the passage or praying it?

Not only are there a great number of ways to pair the various means of Scripture engagement, there is extensive flexibility in what those pairings look like. For instance, on a morning when your time is limited to only five to ten minutes, you might simply write out by hand a verse you would like to commit to memory. On the second day, you then could take your handwritten Scripture and Verse Map it to read it with focus. Alternately, if you have more than five to ten minutes, both steps could be completed in one day. The third day, or whenever time allows, meditate on that same verse.

In times or seasons when you enjoy the luxury of more available time, you could pair even more than two or three of the engaging with Scripture ideas. Recently when my schedule did not allow for participation in an organized Bible study at my church, I gave myself permission to explore engaging with Scripture through a more extensive interweaving.

My chosen passage was the book of Colossians, and my initial engagement with it was pleasure reading. It's a small book so it wasn't a tough stretch to read through it from beginning to end in one sitting. This allowed me to get an overview of the book before digging in. It also blessed me with a time of simply sitting with God and letting His word wash over me. The next day I began writing out the book of Colossians in a composition notebook. I wrote it out Journible-style, on the right-hand page only, skipping two lines between each line of my handwritten text.

Once the entire book had been written out by hand, I went back in and read it with focus using the Read with a Pen (or Lots of Pens). As I worked through the book, I used the left-hand page for any thoughts, reflections, or questions that I had. The left-hand page is also where I placed additional notes from my focused reading if there wasn't enough room on the right-hand page. From time to time, I also selected verses to Verse Map or memorize. The Verse Mapping was also placed on the left-hand page.

Some time ago, I used this same approach with the book of Philippians. The only difference was that I worked chapter by chapter through Philippians. After writing out chapter one, I read it with focus before moving on to chapter two. Since I was working through Philippians in conjunction with a study of the book my small group was doing, I wanted to be prepared for each meeting by working through one chapter at a time.

There are no rules for what your time in the Bible looks like. Make it fit you. Make it fit your purpose.

Personal Reflection

1. What combinations of Read It, Write It, Meditate on It, Memorize It, or Pray It do you see as natural pairings?

2. Describe in detail what two of these pairings would look like as done by you.

3. Go back and look over the Lectio Divina resource (page 92). How do you see the idea of pairing Scripture engagement practices showing up in Lectio Divina?

4. Pray. Ask God to open your understanding to how He has wired you and how this understanding can help you better connect with Him. Then give yourself the permission and the grace to explore various pairings of the Scripture engagement ideas.

11

Nutrition for the Soul

Do you recall our spiritual food metaphor from Chapter 8?

God's Word is our spiritual food, and as such, it must be chewed, digested, and taken into our being in order to provide nourishment. It is simply impossible for us to receive all our required nutrition by skipping meals or gulping our "food" down quickly. Planning and work are required. Time and effort are imperative.

In this book, we have identified five ways to engage the Scripture – Read It, Write It, Meditate on It, Memorize It, and Pray It. Let's be honest, it's one thing to identify. It's quite another to implement. Implementation will only come when we are intentional.

In order to receive the nutrition our soul requires, we must make sure to "eat" our meals.

"Your words were found, and I ate them, and your words became to me a joy and the delight of my heart, for I am called by your name, O LORD, God of hosts."
Jeremiah 15:16

At the same time, it is crucial that we do not gulp our meals but take careful time to chew and digest our "food." This does not come without making our "mealtime" a priority and approaching it with a plan.

There are no limits. There are no restrictions to how we spend our time engaging with God's Word. The important thing is that we do it. Make it your priority to get into the Scripture – *ad fontes* ("to the sources") even if you only have a few minutes. On days when all you have available is ten short minutes, choose one or more of these ideas and engage fully for those ten minutes.

Serious, intense Bible study is greatly to be treasured and something we need to be doing, but it is not always possible. In some seasons, on some days, we simply must figure out how to come to the table and "eat."

My prayer for you as you move forward is that you do so with an understanding that just as we need to choose our reading strategies based on which one best fits our reading purpose, so we need to choose our Scripture engagement method based on which one best fits our current need.

I also pray you will give yourself permission to explore and to discover multiple ways of engaging more fully with God's Word in those seasons when a full-out Bible study isn't possible. May you find strength for your journey, nourishment for your soul, and a deepening relationship with God as you Read, Write, Meditate on, Memorize, and Pray Scripture.

Personal Reflection

1. Commit to the practice of engaging with Scripture through Reading It, Writing It, Meditating on It, Memorizing It, and Praying It. Consider writing out your commitment and signing it, sharing it with a friend and giving them permission to hold you accountable, or making the commitment to God through prayer.

2. Self-reflect. Has intentional time in God's Word been a daily habit? If not, consider scheduling the time for the next three to four weeks as you work to make it a habit. Write it on your calendar or set a reminder alarm.

3. Make a "mealtime" plan for the next week. What passage or passages will you "eat?" How do you plan to chew and digest your "food?"

4. Pray. Thank God for the treasure of His Word and the freedom to "dine" on it. Pray that the Holy Spirit would open the eyes of your heart as you "feast" on Scripture and for the perseverance to follow through on your commitment to engage more deeply with the Bible.

Additional Resources
for
Engaging with Scripture

Tools for Digging Deeper

Having the right tool for the job can make ALL the difference!

A Journaling Bible – These Bibles have wide margins. There are even some where every other page is blank. Inside a journaling Bible are no distracting notes or commentary, only the Word of God.

Online Bible Study Sites - Bible Gateway, Bible Hub, Blue Letter Bible, Bible Study Tools, and others.

An English Dictionary – Bible translators choose English words with great care. Our understanding can be greatly enhanced simply by using an English dictionary.

A Thesaurus – Synonyms and antonyms can also greatly enhance our understanding of a passage.

Bible Commentary – Helps with understanding the background and context of passages.

Concordance – An "exhaustive" concordance lists every occurrence of every word in the Bible.

Maps – A help with all things geographical: locations, distances, proximities, etc.

Cross-references – The verses listed on the pages of your Bible. Cross-references identify commonalities between different parts of the Bible. These are the best way to grasp what a Bible text is saying. "Let Scripture interpret Scripture."

Bible Translations – Sticks closely to the original language – word for word, thought for thought. Answers the question, "What does it say?"

Bible Paraphrases – Man's interpretation and should be used as a commentary. Answers the question, "What does it mean?"

Soul Friend(s) – Helps you pay attention and process your response. Also adds an element of fun!

Scripture Engagement/Journaling Methods – Verse Mapping, Reading with a Pen (or Lots of Pens), Journible-style, Praying Scripture in Color, Lectio Divina, Color Coding, etc.

Engaging the Scripture A-Z

A Simple List

Ask questions.

Boil what you read down to one or two sentences.

Create timelines.

Draw a picture.

Engage in biblical meditation.

Find a quiet place.

Generate lists.

Highlight key words and phrases.

If there is a "therefore," ask what it's there for.

Jot down your thoughts and observations.

Know the context.

Look for patterns.

Memorize verses and passages.

Notice pronouns. When you come to one, substitute your name.

Organize what you have learned.

Pray Scripture.

Question the Scripture's application to your life.

Read and read again.

Share what you have learned.

Talk to God about what you are reading. He is right there with you.

Use tools – dictionaries, cross-references, commentaries, other Bible translations, etc.

Visualize what you are reading.

Write Scripture passages out by hand.

eXtract the Who, What, When, Where, Why, and How.

Yield to the Holy Spirit's leading.

Zap the distractions before you begin.

20 WAYS TO ENGAGE WITH SCRIPTURE

Find a
quiet place.

Prepare ahead.
Remove distractions.

Read and
read AGAIN.

Substitute your
name for pronouns.

Visualize what
you are reading.

Use tools -
dictionaries, etc.

Ask
questions.

Make
lists.

Highlight key words
and phrases.

Look for patterns
and repetitions.

Draw a
picture.

Write your thoughts
and observations.

Create
timelines.

Pray
Scripture.

Memorize verses
and passages.

Rephrase and
summarize.

Organize what you
have learned.

Make
application.

Review the text
and your notes.

Share what you
have learned.

Creative Ways to Engage with the Scripture

Discuss It

When possible join an organized Bible study. Discussions over the meaning and interpretation of the study's passages of Scripture can be a lively way to engage God's Word. Another option is to gather a soul friend or two and create your own Scripture discussion group.

Display It

Whether you purchase it or create it yourself, decorate your home with Scripture. (Or when committing a verse to memory, write it out on a scrap of paper and post it anywhere you will see it often.)

Do It

Don't just hear the Word. Do it! What better way to engage with Scripture than to do?

"He has told you, O man, what is good;
and what does the LORD require of you
but to do justice, and to love kindness,
and to walk humbly with your God?"
Micah 6:8

Dramatize It

Whether spontaneous or professional, dramatizations can help bring Scripture to life. Drama engages our mind and emotions. A worship drama team can help make truth more clear to a congregation by thoughtfully re-enacting a passage through a well-scripted, rehearsed, costumed presentation. As well, a family can bring a Bible narrative to life with an impromptu dramatization during their time of family devotions.

Journal It

Journaling shares many of the same benefits as writing. The practice of journaling Scripture can slow us down, focus our minds, and help us concentrate.

Listen to It

There are several options for listening to the Word. One way is to listen as you read Scripture aloud for yourself. Of course, another option is to listen as someone else reads. There are some wonderful versions available for purchase, but good ones are also available for free. Listening as someone else reads is a great opportunity to hear the Bible when life is busy.

Read It – Interpretively

Leave the monotone behind and add some pizzazz. Capture the meaning of a passage of Scripture with expression, timing, and passion.

Sing It

There's just something about singing that touches the soul. I've even heard singing referred to as the language of thanksgiving. Whether you locate Scripture songs through an internet search or put Scripture to your own made-up tune, sing! The singing of Scripture helps connect our minds and our hearts with a passage. It's also a powerful way to commit Scripture to memory and to pray Scripture.

Hum It

When you can't sing, hum. Perhaps your surroundings don't allow for belting out a song of Scripture. When something a bit more subtle is called for, hum.

Share It

I have a friend who makes it a practice to share the Scripture she is studying with others. Not long ago she was working through one of the Psalms, journible-style, and at the close of each day's study, she sent the day's Scripture passage and her insights to a group of friends via email. Consider sharing one verse a day with at least one other person for the next month.

Sketch It

Depict the main ideas of a passage with simple illustrations or symbols.

Speak It

Make talking with others about Scripture a habit.

Teach It

They say the best way to learn something is to teach it. That certainly makes sense. Teaching others requires that you know the material. To teach with confidence you must go deep, penetrating the text through study and comprehension.

Ideas for Engaging Young Children with Scripture

The Bible is God's gift to all: to you, to your children, to your grandchildren.

In chapter two ("The Struggle is Real"), we considered the very likely possibility that the reason many of us do not know how to engage with Scripture is that we were never taught how do to so.

Consider these ideas for sharing the Bible – not children's Bibles, not only the stories of Sunday School classes – but the full counsel of God's Word with the children in your lives so that this cycle can be broken.

Involve Your Children as Cast Members

As you read the actual Bible narratives with your children, turn your home into a theater. Let each child assume the role of one of the characters, and if you run out of children let them play multiple roles (or grab some stuffed animals and dolls from their rooms.)

Commission Them as Artists

There are many, many passages of Scripture that are story-driven. When you get to these, take the opportunity to activate your children's imaginations.

Give them a sheet of paper and a pencil or some crayons and ask them to draw what they hear.

The act of drawing will engage your children with the text as it is being read. Additionally, the completed drawings will become a reference guide. They will help your children remember the people of the Bible and their stories, help you make connections for your children as you read on, and create opportunities for you to incorporate the gospel into what your children have seen and drawn.

Create a Mural

Involve your entire family in the art-making. Grab some poster board or butcher paper, and as a family, create a mural of what you are reading.

Feed the imaginations of your children as you read by creating your own scenes of what is happening.

Turn the Bible Passage into a Family Research Project

Passages about constructing the tabernacle (Exodus), building the temple (1 Kings), and others of similar nature are often ones we skip over when reading the Bible with children. After all, these passages are what cause even grown adults to abandon yearly reading plans.

When you get to Bible accounts of this nature, increase your children's interest by looking things up. A new furnishing for the tabernacle? An article of priestly clothing? The layout of the temple? Google it or look it up in a reference book. Add to your child's view of the passage by providing visuals as seen through the eyes of an artist.

Shout "Amen"

Genealogies can be tough. All those names… of people you've never heard of. Adults skirt around them. Surely, children won't get anything from them.

Help your children engage with these passages of genealogy and draw their interest by asking them to shout "Amen" each time they hear a name in the very long list that they are familiar with.

> *"Jesus* **("AMEN")**, *when he began his ministry, was about thirty years of age, being the son (as was supposed) of Joseph* **("AMEN")**, *the son of Heli, the son of Matthat, the son of Levi* **("AMEN")**, *the son of Melchi, the son of Jannai, the son of Joseph* **("AMEN")**, *the son of Mattathias, the son of Amos* **("AMEN")**, *the son of Nahum* **("AMEN")**, *the son of Esli, the son of Naggai."*
> Luke 3:23-25 [("AMEN") added for emphasis.]

Play "Banker"

Another idea for engaging with passages of genealogy is to let your children be the "banker" as you read.

Before embarking on your reading of a lengthy genealogy, fill a large container with beads. Then provide each of your children with their own smaller container or cup. Instruct them to take a bead out of the larger container and put it into their own cup every time a person's name is read. When you come to the end of the genealogy, count how many beads are in each cup.

Write Songs

Prior to reading the Bible text together, ask your children to listen for thoughts or phrases that would be a great song title. When you've finished reading your Scripture, add to the fun by writing your own hymn or worship song. Bonus points for verses or phrases that come from your reading passage.

Pray the Scripture

Using the ideas and tips from Chapter Nine (Pray It), model the praying of Scripture for your children as part of your Bible reading. Periodically, allow them to take turns praying the Scripture for themselves.

Encourage Retelling

Before closing your Bible and moving on to other activities, ask your child to retell the reading passage in their own words. This is a wonderful way for you to ascertain what they grasped from the reading and where you may need to make some clarifications.

Let your child know that they will be asked to retell the passage BEFORE you read through it together. This will help them be more engaged with the text and "read" with purpose.

NOTES

Chapter 2

1 LifeWay Research, "American Views on Bible Reading: Representative Survey of 1000 Americans," (http://lifewayresearch.com/wp-content/uploads/2017/04/Sept-2016-American-Views-Bible-Reading.pdf), September 27-October 1, 2016. Accessed October 22, 2018.

2 Martin Luther, *First Principles of the Reformation or the Ninety-Five Theses and the Three Primary Works of Dr. Martin Luther*, Albemarle Street, London, 1883, 82.

Chapter 3

1 Dr. Fergus Macdonald, taken from "Scripture Engagement: What is It?," (https://www.biblegateway.com/resources/scripture-engagement/main/what-is-scripture-engagement), October 22, 2018.

2 Taken from *Soul Nourishment: Satisfying Our Deep Longing for God* by Deborah Haddix, (Anderson, IN: Warner Press, 2018), 43.

3 Taken from *Women of the Word: How to Study the Bible with Both Our Hearts and Our Minds* by Jen Wilkin, © 2014, pp. 31. Used by permission of Crossway, a publishing ministry of Good News Publishers, Wheaton, IL 60187, www.crossway.org.

4 Wilkin, *Women of the Word*, 33.

Chapter 7

1 Taken from *A Puritan Theology: Doctrine for Life* by Joel R. Beeke and Mark Jones, (Grand Rapids, MI: Reformation Heritage Books, 2012), 2139-2140.

2 Some content taken from *Spiritual Disciplines for the Christian Life* by Donald S. Whitney. Copyright © 2014, p. 105. Used by permission of NavPress. All rights reserved. Represented by Tyndale House Publishers, Inc.

3 Beeke and Jones, *A Puritan Theology*, 2169-2171.

Chapter 8

1 Dallas Willard, taken from "Spiritual Formation in Christ for the Whole Life and Whole Person," *Vocatio*, Vol. 12, no 2, Spring, 2001, 7.

2 Taken from *An Approach to Extended Memorization of Scripture* by Dr. Andrew Davis (Ambassador International: Kindle Edition, April 7, 2014), 10.

Chapter 9

1 Taken from *Praying the Scriptures: A Field Guide for Your Spiritual Journey* by Evan B. Howard, © 1999, pp. 11. Used by permission of InterVarsity Press, Downers Grove, IL 60515, www.ivpress.com.

2 Taken from *Praying in Color: Drawing a New Path to God* by Sybil MacBeth, (Brewster, MA: Paraclete Press, 2013), 19-23.

OTHER RESOURCES BY DEBORAH HADDIX

Soul Nourishment: Satisfying Our Deep Longing for God – is a gentle reminder of the importance of soul care. It is also a handbook for today's busy woman filled with a multitude of easy, ready-to-use resources to bring refreshment on the journey. This 2-color book offers a multitude of ways to intentionally nourish and care for our soul including: prayer practices, using scripture, building relationships, listening, & solitude.

Praying with Purpose: Taking Your Prayer Life from Vague to Victorious— Prayer is the most precious gift we can give our loved ones, and this book provides us with a wonderful roadmap for enjoying and sharing a focused and creative prayer life. For those who often pray vague prayers, this book has many suggestions and resources compiled to encourage and inspire victorious praying. *Praying With Purpose* includes creative and real world methods for a variety of different types of prayer and prayer topics.

Journaling for the Soul: A Handbook — The busyness of life has made its migration into the depths of our being, squeezing God out. Our soul cries out but the noise of life keeps it from being heard. *Journaling for the Soul* helps eliminate the hurry, brings quiet for hearing, and creates much needed space for soul work. This book includes a wide range of different methods to suit a variety personalities or seasons of life and topics: gratitude, simplicity, vision boards, timelines, journaling for friends, fears, self-reflection, attributes of God, names of Christ.

Digging Deeper KIDS (3 Options)

- Digging Deeper KIDS Methods includes 9 different techniques for helping children engage with the Word of God.

- Kids' Journaling Templates are perfect for the child who is intimidated by a blank page or as "training wheels" for the Digging Deeper Kids Methods.

- The Digging Deeper Kids BUNDLE includes both The Digging Deeper Methods AND The Digging Deeper Journaling Templates.

For more information on these and other resources by Deborah Haddix, visit deborahhaddix.com.

Made in the USA
Columbia, SC
25 May 2019